THE SUPER ATTORNEY

A Step by Step Guide to Growing Your Law Firm without Working Harder or Raising Your Fees

Big Mouth Marketing

Published in United States in 2018 by Big Mouth Marketing
Copyright © Big Mouth Marketing 2018

Second Edition

Printed and bound in USA by Selby Marketing

Big Mouth Marketing
Address:
4400 North Scottsdale Rd, #9-732
Scottsdale, AZ 85251

www.bigmouthmarketing.co

Testimonials

"Gary has been very helpful in my understanding of what he can do for my law practice. He spends the time and effort to provide you with an understanding and level of comfort before you invest a single dollar."

–Frank Piscitelli

"The folks at BMM have been absolutely wonderful to work with. Very knowledgeable about marketing topics that have helped my business succeed in a short period of time. Very innovative ideas that they help to implement, which I certainly wouldn't have thought of or executed on my own, especially with the little bandwidth I have. Great experience and results!"

–Brint Hiatt

"Gary has been a great person to work with. He has a tremendous understanding of marketing and a lot of experience, yet he's willing to take time to personally help by sharing his masterful insight. I look forward to growing and learning more from him. I would recommend him with more than 5 stars!"

–Jay

"Gary knows his stuff, and I especially appreciate his transparency about his pricing and processes. Few folks in this space have his creativity and diligence in marketing for lawyers."

–Jarome

"It was very helpful to speak with Gary and to learn from his experiences. His insight and expertise was very enlightening. I am going to make some major changes in my firm's plan because of the call. I recommend every legal entrepreneur take the time to chat with him."

–Jon

"Gary has some great insight on legal marketing!"

–Vik P

"Gary is probably the most important connection I have made in the last 10 years. He has become the guru on the mountaintop for all of our legal marketing needs. His understanding of attraction marketing using the crocodile brain and mass marketing system have proven to deliver amazing results. He has been able to help us create better sales processes, attract better clients and grow our legal financing platform by leaps and bounds. Gary is like a college professor that can take complex subjects and simplify them in a way anyone could understand. 10/10 would recommend if you are looking for more clients, who are ready to hire you before they ever meet you."

–Jason B

"Marisssa and Kenyon at Big Mouth Marketing gave me a terrific understanding as we walked through the initial process after joining their team to assist my Law Practice. Happy to Rate '5 stars.'"

–Vera B

"Thank you Gary! Very informative and we look forward to working with you to accelerate our law firm."

–Steven M

"Gary Musler at Big Mouth is one of the most brilliant copy writers I've ever met. We refer them a lot of clients because they know how to get results with adwords. The last lawyer I sent to Gary just weeks ago told me had 30 phone calls for $2000 in ad spend. That's in 2017 where some lawyer can't even buy a single click at $60, let alone a phone call from a red hot client."

–Frankie F

"I am impressed with the level of knowledge of Gary and how informative he was about the marketing process. I am eager to become a client and would definitely refer him to other attorneys regarding building their businesses and self-branding.

This is the key most important step. Start your foundation."

–Tia H

"Gary has done a great job marketing our law firm.
We would recommend Gary and his team to anyone
needing to enhance their internet presence."

–Cory S

"Gary and Dave have been a huge help to my business and
marketing plan. Gary is very honest, personable and very
talented/successful in legal marketing. I've been practicing
law in Scottsdale for 25 years and get calls all the time from
legal marketers and I've tried my share—Gary is by far
the best I have found and I highly recommend him."

–Donald Y

"I'm very impressed with Big Mouth Marketing!! Gary and
his team have completed design and implantation of our new
campaign in timely and professional manner. We converted our
first lead on the first day of launch, which paid for the first month!
Looking forward to the future relationship with Big Mouth."

–Don T

"Gary and his team at Big Mouth are absolutely phenomenal
to work with. Their customer service is exceptional—
always available for a call, email, etc. whenever I have a
question. I highly recommend Big Mouth Marketing!"

–Manal C

"I contacted Big Mouth Marketing for a marketing consultation
and spoke with Gary Musler who did not 'sell' me his services,
unlike others I have contacted. Rather, we discussed the specific
needs of my law firm, practice areas, past marketing efforts
and marketing budget. Gary was candid in our discussion
about my current website and the unsuccessful marketing
plans I had subscribed to over the past three years. He is very
knowledgeable and explained the reasons the prior plans did

not work. I am so busy with my law practice, I had simply relied on the expertise of these other marketing companies to my firm's detriment. Gary made recommendations for a solid marketing plan for my law firm. I truly appreciate Gary's honesty and believe he has my firm's best interest at heart."

–Heidi H

"For those of us learning how to improve our marketing, BMM offers up great, fresh, usable ideas, and case studies with plenty of detail, plus usable tactics/strategies that I can actually put to use. Thanks."

–Jim M

"The attention to detail is incredible. These guys (Peter and Gary) are terrific. They delve into areas of marketing that includes comments on the structure of the article as well as how to best tweak curiosity so the intended recipient reads the article. Thanks very much to both of you for so many little gems to help me in doing this effectively."

–Joseph T

"As a PI attorney you know I get marketed to all the time and unfortunately over the years I never found that elite marketing expert that really knows exactly how to market and grow my law practice. Fortunately, that all changed the day I met Gary and started working with Big Mouth Marketing. From the beginning Gary was very patient and it was clear that he was laser focused on my best interest, a refreshing change from others that just wanted to sell me something! He took the time to learn about my practice in great detail. It was abundantly clear from day one that his goal was to help grow my practice. Any attorney that is ready to grow their practice owes it to themselves to have a conversation with a true marketing expert and a gracious genuine man."

–Don S

"Going from having zero knowledge within marketing to knowing how to write articles, write attractive headlines, deploy a strategic marketing campaign, advertise on any platform *and in any media all within a few weeks ain't bad. Immense insight into marketing. Peter and Gary are the bee's knees!"*

–Matt L

"This is what I've missing all along. I knew more needed to be done but didn't have the know-how. Get me in front of a qualified prospect and I'll work my magic but the marketing stuff should be left to the pro's. Gary and his team are true pro's! 3 things I'll say about his strategy and execution. WOW, just WOW!!!!"

–Ryan E

"Peter and Gary are very interested in making sure that all our questions are answered. The content is incredible and very well presented. If I was to use but one word to describe the experience it would be OVER THE TOP (sorry that is 3 words !!!)"

–Joe T

"Great content as always. The exciting thing is how easily I can start to see how each strategy can work (and be implemented) with well thought out rationale (and proof) behind each one. The case study critiques are massively valuable and good to see real-time evaluations with structured recommendations to take action from."

–Chris C

"Big Mouth is absolutely incredible and I wouldn't even consider using another firm for Internet marketing. They absolutely exceeded my expectations and they were VERY upfront and straight forward from the get go. Gary and Dave are amazing and you can tell that they are truly passionate about what they do and helping their clients. Thank you so much guys! I am a client for life."

–Michael I

"Just talked to Gary. He was very helpful and friendly. This is a great company and I am very happy with their professionalism and wisdom. They are the way to go!"

–Greg G

"Peter and Gary provide friendly, descriptive, and easily-digestible comprehensive content regarding simple to use, but difficult to master techniques for growing your business by utilizing untapped potential. Fantastic guys, great calls. I've only been to 5 of these webinars so far, and I'm absolutely hooked. It makes my morning to get some fresh marketing inspiration from the guys at Big Mouth."

–Mippi M

"The latest call came out of nowhere and brought a whole new prospective on marketing strategy. This is what Big Mouth does they keep on pushing you in different directions and show you that marketing isn't a one trick pony!"

–Bill K

CONTENTS

INTRODUCTION

Will You Be an Attorney Who Falls Behind or Who Embraces the Coming Change?

IN 1800 A VERY poor boy named John Bullough was born in Westhoughton, a small parish town in northern England.

When he grew up, he was often described as a simple-minded weaver.

Working long hours, for low pay, doing repetitive work, he was one of society's downtrodden.

He was one among 200,000 handloom weavers in England at the time.

Later in life, a dozen or so of those 200,000 handloom weavers hatched a plan to murder John.

He was forced to leave his home.

Interestingly, the reason why they were trying to murder John Bullough all those years ago has everything to do with you growing your law firm today.

You see, in 1826 there was a protest against the new machinery known as the power loom.

It was more efficient and didn't require as many workers.

John was soon to be out of a job, along with hundreds of thousands of other workers.

Instead of worrying about it, he decided to embrace the coming wave of change.

While the protest turned into a riot and the twenty ring leaders were arrested, John was quietly working on an even better version of the loom.

He made it more efficient and even added safety features.

Soon he was a founding partner of the biggest manufacturer in the whole of the England.

This simple-minded man, with barely two pennies to rub together, transformed the world.

However, he upset people who were left behind, which is why they tried to have him murdered. Luckily, they failed.

Clothes became cheaper and more affordable for everyone. Nothing would ever be the same.

While you are reading the very words on this page, something very similar is unfolding in the legal industry (especially in America).

There will be two types of attorneys in the near future.

The first will embrace the future and grow their law firm.

The second will initially stay stagnant and then slowly fall behind.

As technology and methods of acquiring clients moves forward, the lawyers who embrace it will quickly have a distinct advantage.

John Bullough wasn't the only one to embrace change. His factory employed 6,000 workers, who got paid handsomely.

He supplied other factories with his looms, and THOSE businesses grew exponentially.

Every single time people embrace the coming waves of change, they have a much better chance of turning it into fortunes.

However, please do not misinterpret the contents of this book. I am not guaranteeing your future or promising wealth.

All I can give you are the facts as I see them.

After helping over 550 law firms grow, 1.5 million leads in various areas, and 5,000 marketing tests, my team and I tend to keep our finger on the pulse.

And what makes a law firm grow today is completely different from ten years ago.

While you are reading this book, there are "Super Attorneys" out there who are making use of these growth strategies.

Although to the outside world, these super attorneys seem to be "lucky" or "clever," the truth is very different.

Each of these steps is simple and has been thoroughly tested and planned by pioneers in the industry.

There isn't any guesswork involved. You simply implement the steps outlined, *the very same steps the super attorneys have taken*, and monitor the results.

Unlike John, you don't have to invent anything. You simply have to embrace the new growth tools available to you, like the manufacturers who used John's new equipment.

Even though it is simple, very few attorneys are willing to make the small adjustments required to reach the next level in service and income.

That's the **good** news. The attorneys who act now will quickly jump to the front of the pack, while other attorneys dither and hesitate. You simply need to pick the side you want to be part of.

There is a sad truth that most attorneys are ignoring.

Just like the 200,000 handloom weavers who lost their jobs, attorneys up and down America are about to get a wakeup call.

In this book I'll be talking about the coming changes that are going to hit the legal industry.

Some of these changes will spell the death of many law offices yet will enrich others beyond their wildest dreams.

Change is coming, and there is nothing you or I can do to stop it. All we can do is prepare.

Some of it has already started happening.

Since 1960 the IRS has collected and published income levels for solo attorneys.

Things are not looking good.

In 1988 the average attorney took home $70,747 per year in today's money.

And by 2012 that figure had dropped down to $49,130.

That is a scary 30% decrease in real earning power.

When I discovered this shocking information, I decided to put my research team to task.

And what we uncovered is nothing short of alarming.

However, like I already said, this is actually **good news** for those attorneys who are willing to embrace the changing environment and invest in their own success.

This book is a great start.

First, we'll explore some of the rapid changes that are already underway and how they will affect you.

Then we'll move onto the only two ways to grow your law firm during this period and the different strategies you can use to grow rich.

Let's get stuck in.

CHAPTER 1

The Coming Waves to Hit the Legal Industry

"Change is the law of life. And those who look only to the past or present are certain to miss the future."

John F. Kennedy (1917–1963), Thirty-fifth President of the USA

ALMOST NOBODY HAS helped more attorneys change with the times than Alexis Neely. She's even been featured on Good Morning America, CNBC, and The Today Show.

When I spoke to her, she gave me the unfiltered truth.

*"I've been training lawyers now for more than 10 years, and I have seen a far greater willingness to change than I've ever seen before. And I think that that is because **the smart lawyers see the writing on the wall,** which is that the way we've learned to practice law is no longer going to work to allow us to have the lives that we want to have. And that if they want to have great lives, they're going to need to do things differently than the way they've*

*done them in the past, in the ways they've been taught to do them. So, I think we are actually in the mix of a huge industry-wide change, and the smart lawyers are getting on board with that, and **the lawyers that are going to be left behind are remaining resistant to that change.**"*

Just after Christmas, eighteen-year-old Louis Cryer's life was changed forever.

It took just a matter of seconds for a body of water to burst through the wall of the hotel.

It was December 26, 2004, and he was on vacation with his mother and brother.

They were lucky enough to escape to a temple on higher ground. Any closer to the water and they could have been one of the 240,000 who lost their lives that day.

A 9.0 magnitude earthquake occurred in the Indian Ocean near the west coast of Sumatra.

The violent movement of the tectonic plates displaced an enormous amount of water and sent shock waves in every direction.

At the same time, Kay Howells was snorkeling off of Phi Phi Lei, Thailand.

The water receded, and the local Thai family who manned the boat called everybody back.

They quickly recognized the danger and repositioned the boat far away from the shore.

Kay Howells recalls seeing people getting swept away by the coming wave. Her group, on the other hand, were safe and completely unharmed.

The same was true for the Onge tribe.

They have lived on Little Andaman (an island) for between 30,000 and 50,000 years, and although they are on the verge of extinction, almost all of the one hundred or so people left seem to have survived the December 26 earthquake and the devastating waves that followed.

Why?

Well, they felt the earth quake and saw the water receding.

Stories passed down from thousands of years ago told them a big wall of water was coming.

They fled to the higher ground deep in the forest. Their settlements were destroyed, but they all survived.

Others who migrated from Southeast Asia weren't so wise. They didn't understand what was going on.

When I read about all of these stories, I realized that there were three types of people who were affected by the horrible events of that day.

1. The ones who were swept away

2. The ones who were lucky enough to be on safer ground already and could quickly escape

3. The ones who were given the knowledge and used it to survive

When you think about it, those three categories apply to almost everything in life.

Change is constant. It comes in waves, and some people get swept away by it, often through no fault of their own.

There was no way for them to know. There was no way for them to escape. It was an impossible situation.

According to a Delloitte Insight report published in February 2016, over 100,000 jobs in the legal sector have a high chance of disappearing in the next few years.

Swept away by a wave of change.

In fact, there will be three major waves to hit the legal industry—each one worse than the one before.

Those who know about the waves, and which actions to take to prepare, will survive (and even thrive).

Those who do not know about them will find themselves stuck, without any good options.

So what are the waves, and how can you prepare?

Before I get into that, I have to clarify something.

This book isn't meant to scare you into submission. Nor am I here to spell the doom of all things legal.

This book is about growing your law firm and increasing your wealth as an attorney.

And accordingly, I won't spend one hundred pages going through all of the research and evidence there is for the coming waves of change.

Instead, I will give you a brief overview coupled with references for further reading, if you wish.

So without further delay, let's dive into the first wave of change.

WAVE #1: TOO MANY LAWYERS, TOO FEW JOBS

The first wave is actually already here. At a quick glance you'll probably conclude that things *"are not that bad."*

Yet, if you read the words on this page carefully, you'll see how the coming legal crisis has already started.

For example, Whittier Law School in California is shutting its doors. And it is just one of many.

"We were completely caught off guard," Kristopher Escobedo, a second-year student and incoming student body president at the Costa Mesa, California, school, told the *Los Angeles Times*. *"It was almost like an ambush."*

Future lawyers, heed this. Whittier's demise could be a sign of things to come.

According to Michael Horn from the Clayton Christensen Institute, Whittier Law School is not an isolated case.

Most non-elite law schools are hanging on for dear life to try and thin out the heard.

The reason is simple. The percentage of law school graduates with employment has dropped by 5% in the last few years.

What does this even mean?

Well, simply put, the number of attorneys practicing law in the U.S. has fallen by 5%.

And it isn't because there are less attorneys.

It is because top law firms are taking a bigger share of the pie than ever.

They are out on the water with the biggest boat, and they know the wave is coming.

However, 5% doesn't seem too bad. That is true, until you consider that the economy has been expanding for almost ten straight years and unemployment everywhere has fallen to record lows.

A 5% drop in employment is normal during a recession, but not during one of the longest economic booms in U.S. history.

And don't be fooled, the rate of employment for attorneys doesn't simply affect law school graduates. It has a direct correlation with how many clients you get and how much they spend with you.

This is especially going to bite in the next downturn. That's when the second wave is going hit, and it will hit HARD.

WAVE #2: HUNDREDS OF THOUSANDS OF NEWER, MORE INNOVATIVE ATTORNEYS WILL TRY AND STEAL YOUR CLIENTS

Wave #1 will seem tame compared to wave #2.

Inflation in legal fees has outstripped general inflation for a while now, and a lot of people are struggling to afford the costs.

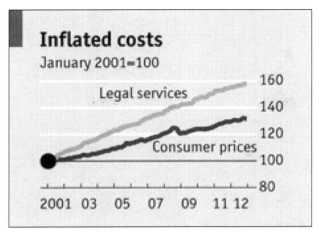

Source *The Economist*: https://www.economist.com/news/leaders/21571141-cheaper-legal-education-and-more-liberal-rules-would-benefit-americas-lawyersand-their

To make matters worse, legal costs in the U.S. are staggeringly high compared to other countries.

Large corporations are well aware of that fact and are taking action.

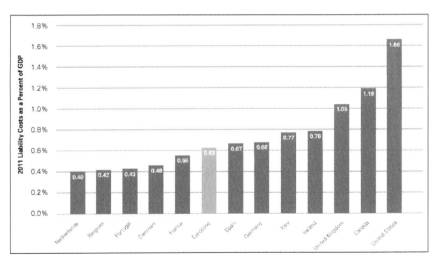

The U.S. has the highest liability costs as a percentage of its economy.

And even more startling, it is 2.6 times higher than the countries within the Eurozone.

Even though this is the case, I actually believe you should be charging more for your services.

In a minute I'll show you how to do exactly that WITHOUT losing any new clients.

So whatever you do, keep reading.

The chart you see above was an international study published for corporations.

And according to Greg Toppo from *USA Today*, corporate legal departments and law firms are under growing pressure to cut costs.

They are spending vast sums of money on automation technology to replace their more junior attorneys.

Not only is the percentage of attorneys employed falling in a growing economy, there is about to be a tidal wave of young, smart, and hungry attorneys coming after your clients.

This especially puts the smaller law firms in jeopardy. In the past, competing with new law school graduates was easy.

Although there were a lot of them, they were inexperienced and naive.

The young attorneys from the corporate sector will have experience in one of the most cutthroat industries out there.

Their attention to detail and ambition will be difficult to match. The hypercompetitive culture of the corporate world will finally spill over from the cities to the entire country.

In fact, it is my opinion that as the corporate world starts to shed legal jobs, the average attorney is going to face stiffer competition **than at any point in history.**

Unlike most solo practitioners, the corporate attorneys are used to working 18 hours a day without weekends.

Most established attorneys will retaliate in the worst way.

They will try and match the work ethic of the younger corporate lawyers. They will cut their prices and work harder.

That flame will be rapidly extinguished. Many thousands of established law offices will go under.

The answer doesn't lie in working harder and burning yourself out; it lies in working smarter.

You'll discover exactly how in this book.

However, this is only wave #2. Wave #3 will crush the dreams of attorneys who aren't prepared for what's coming.

Before I reveal what wave #3 is, just remember that there is a bright light at the end of this dark tunnel.

Attorneys who take the steps to prepare won't simply survive; you will thrive in the coming waves of change.

WAVE #3: ATTORNEYS' "BREAD-AND-BUTTER" JOBS WILL RAPIDLY BE ELIMINATED

During the industrial revolution, a flood of processes and technology eliminated millions of jobs—and created many millions more.

The steam engine kick-started everything in 1775, from trains to ships.

The cotton gin sped up clothing and linen production with its invention in 1793.

The telegraph streamlined communication across long distances in 1844.

And countless other disruption created winners and losers during the Industrial Revolution.

In the next few years, a similar wave will cause this kind of disruption. Not even attorneys will be safe.

There is a flood of technology coming into the market that is designed to replace the activities of an attorney.

At first, this seems ridiculous. Yet, in San Francisco, there is a company that is teaching an AI (named iCEO) to replace middle management in large firms.

The AI breaks all of management's tasks into smaller tasks and outsources them to cheaper locations.

It then monitors the workers and learns how to do their jobs, eventually firing everyone and taking care of the tasks itself.

A single program is able to do this. It will constantly learn from different industries and inputs, simultaneously upgrading itself across sectors.

The same will happen to attorneys.

According to Dan Mangan from CNBC, lawyers could be the next profession to be replaced by computers.

He demonstrates how this is already happening.

For example, LawGeex is a computer program. It can take a new contract, one that it's never seen before, read it, and then compare it to a database of every similar contract that it's seen in the past.

That's kind of like showing a contract to over a million attorneys, having them analyze it, and suggesting changes, all within a split second.

And this wave is just starting. A lot more is coming.

The legal sector has been slow to change. However, when the change comes it will be rapid.

The horse and cart was used for thousands of years until, what seemed like overnight, it was replaced by the car.

For example.

ROSS Intelligence makes a legal research platform based on IBM's "thinking" computer system called Watson.

It is being used by some of the world's largest law firms, including Dentons and Latham & Watkins.

Andrew Arruda, ROSS Intelligence's CEO and co-founder, said his company *"is working with lawyers from every type of organization—in-house, big, medium, small, solo [practitioners]—as well as law schools and bar associations."*

So firms up and down the country are gunning for the jobs of ordinary attorneys. You may be one of them.

In a minute I'll show you exactly how to insulate yourself from this coming wave of automation. In fact, you'll be able to thrive while other attorneys go bust.

And they WILL go bust.

Don't forget what I mentioned earlier. Delloitte Insight estimates 100,000 attorneys will lose their jobs. That includes small law firms too.

While that is going on, there will be a handful of attorneys who greatly benefit from this change.

Just like the winners and losers in the industrial revolution.

This was confirmed by Sofia Lingos, an attorney and member of the board at the Technology Resource Center of the American Bar Association (ABA).

At a <u>roundtable</u> discussion, she was asked if attorneys should be afraid of Artificial Intelligence or embrace it?

She calmly stated, "Both."

She continued to explain that the attorneys who embrace the changes, rapidly coming to the industry, *"will flourish."*

Others will surely suffer.

HOW TO THRIVE DURING THE COMING CHAOS

When John Bullough's invention was blamed for the loss of 200,000 handloom jobs, there were protests, lawsuits, and riots.

In the end, those who opposed the coming technological and social changes did not win.

No matter how much they felt like it was unfair.

No matter how much they tried to keep the status quo.

Nothing would save them from the change, except to change themselves.

The 2004 tsunami did the same.

It was a wave that nobody could stop.

Let's imagine people lined up at the beaches of Phuket, Thailand, and picketed the coming tsunami.

They yelled at the ocean and threatened it, saying things like, *"I will never swim in you again!"*

Even the idea of such a thing would be laughable and unimaginable.

The wave would come nonetheless, and those people who are protesting it would tragically be swept away.

Yet, many attorneys are doing exactly that.

According to Thomson Reuters in their **Legal Department 2025 Series**:

> *The legal market has undergone fundamental and permanent changes since the global economic meltdown of 2008. From the influx of millennials into the workplace to the use of artificial intelligence, legal process outsourcers and alternative providers, new market drivers are shaping the legal profession and forcing change.*
>
> *Such dramatic shifts can be disorienting, yet the benefits of effective change management can't be overstated....With so much at stake, why aren't more lawyers at the forefront of technology and innovation?*

I have spoken to thousands of attorneys on a one-to-one basis the last several years.

In fact, I still speak to at least ten new attorneys, who I have never met before, every single month.

My experiences with a lot of these attorneys reflect the conclusions of mountains of research conducted by Thomson Reuters.

Many attorneys are resistant to the coming waves of change.

Yet, it isn't truly the attorneys who are at fault here.

Just like the innocent bystanders who were swept away by the tsunami, nobody has made a concerted effort to prepare attorneys for the change.

In fact, I would go as far as to say that the ABA and law schools across the country have unknowingly made attorneys resistant to what's coming.

And many law firms will go bankrupt because of it.

Let me explain.

You probably already know that the legal profession relies on precedent.

The very nature of law largely relies on the guidance from previous case law or interpretation of the intention of legislation.

The entire industry is also very risk averse.

Legal memos will often contain incredibly long lists of what could potentially go wrong.

Neither of those things are inherently bad. In fact, they are a requirement if you want to be good at your job.

Law schools who do not teach this way of practicing law are doing their students a disservice.

However, it embeds a culture of "doing what was done before" in all aspects of practicing law.

Yet growing your law firm during a period of technological change requires a completely different outlook.

According to the same Reuters research:

> Another factor is the legal education system, which hasn't evolved in decades, despite declining law school enrollment and more limited job prospects. Technology and the business side of law are overlooked; law schools continue to emphasize litigation and the Socratic method of instruction, instead of the competencies lawyers need to be successful in this changing environment, such as skills in data analysis, coding, statistics and marketing.

The difference between thriving in the industry and *"doing a good job for clients"* are two different things.

Don't get me wrong. Doing a good job for clients is essential when it comes to running a successful practice. It will be even more so during the coming waves.

However, in business it is known as a **Service Qualifier**, not a **Service Winner**.

It is kind of like walking into a restaurant and ordering a meal.

You expect the food to be decent and fresh, the staff to be friendly, the restaurant to be clean, and the price to reflect the quality.

We can all agree that is what is required from a good restaurant.

However, we EXPECT those things. For the restaurant to even qualify to get our business, it needs to be a good restaurant.

Those things are **service qualifiers**.

A **service WINNER** is something that wins over customers.

For this, the restaurant needs to do something different.

The same is true of attorneys.

Your clients expect you to be able to do your job well. It doesn't win them over. It is simply something that qualifies you to have them as a client.

What wins them over is going above and beyond. We'll be discussing simple ways of doing this later on in the book.

It is actually very simple and will make your life easier.

Hopefully now you and I can agree that doing a good job is essential to surviving; however, it will not help you to thrive.

A lot of attorneys mistakenly believe that it does.

When I talk to attorneys about this, they usually cut right to the chase:

So Gary, what is needed for me to thrive during the coming changes?

The answer, luckily, is incredibly simple. Maybe too simple for most attorneys to get their heads around.

As a lawyer, the answers to legal questions come in the form of long verdicts and interpretations.

The same is not true in the world of business and growth.

Often the most elegant solutions are the simplest ones.

Most attorneys have what psychologists call a **Fixed Mindset**. Instead, they require a **Growth Mindset**.

Psychologist Carol Dweck explained this in *Stanford Magazine*:

> *For them, each task is a challenge to their self-image, and each setback becomes a personal threat. So they pursue only activities at which they're sure to shine – and avoid the sorts of experiences necessary to grow and flourish in any endeavor.*

This creates a fear of failure, which is reinforced by the bar and a school system that praised intelligence and discouraged risk taking.

According to the Harvard Business Review:

> *People with growth mindsets (incremental theorists) see outcomes not as evidence of who they are but as evidence of what they could improve upon in the future and what challenges they could overcome.*

It is kind of like when smartphones first came out.

Instead of getting angry that there is a better phone out there than yours, simply get the new phone and use its new features to make your life better.

You don't let the outcome, *the old phone*, dictate who you are. You use it as evidence of what challenges the new phone can overcome.

That's a growth mindset.

Old outcomes shouldn't dictate the way you run yourself or your law practice.

Remember, at the beginning of this chapter we observed that there are three kinds of people:

1. The ones who get swept away

2. The ones who get lucky enough to be on safer ground already and could quickly escape

3. The ones were given the knowledge and used it to survive

The third kind have a growth mindset and will use it to survive—and even thrive.

You simply have to decide which camp you want to belong to.

According to Ken Hardison, founder of the Personal Injury Lawyers Marketing & Management Association (known by those who work with him as the 'millionaire maker') there is a good reason why attorneys are resisting to the change that's coming.

> *"I think the one reason is because they're skeptical of change and they're skeptical of everything because when you go to law school, they teach you to be skeptical and think about the worst thing that can happen and we're governed by the rule of law and that's steadfast. And so, we like rules and we like to keep the rules and stay with the rules. And nobody likes changes because it's outside of your comfort zone and you're scared of it because you really don't know what it's going to bring."*

The next few chapters will give you all of the tools you need to crush the coming change and prepare yourself for the riches it will bring.

So, whatever you do, keep reading.

CHAPTER 2

The Only Two Ways to Grow Your Law Firm

"Twenty years from now you will be more disappointed by the things you did not do than by the ones you did. So…sail away from the safe harbor. Explore. Dream. Discover."

Samuel Langhorne Clemens (1835–1910), Better known by his pen name, Mark Twain

THERE ARE TWO attorneys from Colorado.

Both went to the same law school at the University of Colorado Boulder.

They had similar backgrounds, and a lot of people would mistake them for brothers.

As far as people could judge, their prospects out in the world were equally good.

One of them amassed a fortune and became the most successful lawyer in the state.

The other one went broke a couple of years ago. He has had "hard luck" the family explains. He "never seemed to catch hold after law school."

The successful attorney didn't seem to have the same problem. He simply sailed his way to the top. Everything he touched turned into an instant success.

I spoke to this successful attorney (who wanted to remain anonymous) and asked him about his secret to success.

Before he even spoke, I almost knew what he was going to say, word for word.

Generating 1.5 million leads for attorneys of various levels has allowed me to gain access to some of the most successful lawyers in America.

And there seems to be a single common thread that binds them.

Even if they don't know about one another, the most successful lawyers all have something in common.

They stick to a set of "rules" or a "blueprint" of sorts. This blueprint is pretty much the same every single time.

Even brand-new attorneys, fresh out of law school, can turn themselves into a huge success if they follow the principles outlined here.

Unfortunately, there is a chasm.

A huge and expanding chasm between the super successful attorneys, and the ones "just getting by."

Even attorneys pulling in $500,000 to $2 million per year have more room for growth than they can possibly imagine.

I am talking about the super attorneys. The ones who seem to have more free time, more success, and more golf practice than anyone else.

This will be true, even during the coming waves of change, because they understand that there are only two ways to grow their law firm.

And when pursuing growth, they have a relentless focus on those two things.

1. Get **more income** from existing clients.

2. Get **more clients**.

Those are truly the only two ways to grow your law firm. However, there are some inherent problems with growth.

Let's take the first one: *Get more income from existing clients.*

The logic is simple.

If each client paid you more, then your income will grow.

There is no disputing it.

However, I'm sure you see the problem staring us all in the face.

We've already established that attorneys are expensive for average Americans, and fees have risen over time much faster than inflation.

Is raising our fees really the answer?

No, not necessarily. Let me quickly demonstrate one way you could increase your income from existing clients.

In 1904 there were 175 cars sold in America.

The cheapest car at the time was the Ford Model A, at $800.

The average American earned $200–400 per year. So, the cheapest car was well outside of their price range.

The car industry back then faced the same problem the legal industry does now.

Yet, the new manufacturing methods meant that more cars had to be sold.

The dealerships had two options:

1. Get all the cash up front or

2. Extend terms and take on the risk themselves.

A few years later, a man named William Durant, the co-founder of General Motors, came up with a great idea.

He would finance the cars to the dealers, who then would finance them to customers.

In 1919 he opened the first branch of the General Motors Acceptance Corp., and by 1928, less than ten years later, they had financed over 4 million cars.

That's a far cry from the first 175 in 1904.

The car industry grew enormous and created some of the wealthiest men in the world.

Cheap cars and expensive cars became affordable to most people.

The manufacturers, like Ford and GM, are the same as the legal system.

The dealerships are the same as the law firms.

The legal system is putting out the product, and the law office is helping clients to get hold of the product and use it.

The car industry, like many others, used financing to grow. And the same is happening in the legal industry.

Up until recently, attorneys could not offer financing to their clients. The process was complicated, and a lot of the time it violated bar rules.

However, it is now possible to raise your fees, become more affordable, and get all of the cash for your services up front.

All without breaking bar rules.

The attorneys who are taking advantage of this new way of servicing clients have reaped the rewards.

Later on in the book I'll get into the specifics; however, let me demonstrate how this increases the income you gain from existing clients.

When you extend terms as an attorney, you try to get as much up front as possible. A lot of the time this will be 50%.

The rest of the payments will come in installments.

You have no guarantees that the full amount will be paid. You cannot take legal action against a client for not paying. Your insurance company will also hit back.

According to L Squared Insurance, if you did go after clients for not paying fees, you would face higher malpractice insurance premiums.

I asked several attorneys how many of the clients they extend terms to honor them fully.

So far, the total is a staggeringly low 25%.

Now imagine this scenario.

The client walks through your door, and they pay you everything up front.

They get to pay small monthly installments to a finance company, while you get to work knowing that the money is safely in your bank account.

All of a sudden, you'll find yourself with more cash, higher income, and better client relationships, without having raised your fees.

The bar approves of this method, and insurance companies won't raise your premiums.

Like I said, I will explain how this is possible in detail in the next chapter.

For now, my point is this. Super attorneys up and down America are deploying these very tactics to outmaneuver the average law office.

They are razor-focused on the only two ways to grow their law firm.

One of these attorneys, who I have had the great privilege of working closely with, explains it best.

His name is Zaid Abdullah, and he is fast becoming one hell of a successful super attorney.

He runs an incredible firm in Illinois. The last time I spoke to him he told me this:

> "My comfort level is through the roof. I mean, you know, you still got to work hard, you got to still push more. And as you grow your expenses grow, and you have to grow your revenue. I mean, it's always a battle of growing the revenue, but the fact that I know that I have money coming at the end of the month, that I know my bills are going to be paid, I can give my family whatever they want. I mean it gives me a comfort level through the roof. My legal work is better than before because, you know, I don't have too many financial issues."

This is but one example of the first way: **getting more income from existing clients**.

There will be many more.

Including practice-specific topics on the second way of growing your law firm.

You'll discover how the top **Divorce** attorneys get high paying clients, as well as **DUI**, **Personal Injury**, **Immigration**, and more.

You'll see under the hood of their newly financed campaigns, and you'll know exactly how to replicate their results.

Now that you know what the super attorney focusses on, you can join them. Start by reading the very next chapter in this book.

CHAPTER 3

How to Get Clients to Afford Your Fees & Get Paid Up Front While Increasing Your Income

"Whether you think you can, or think you can't—you're right."

Henry Ford (1863–1947), Founder of the Ford Motor Company

IN MARCH 2012, John M. peddled as fast as he could.

He'd never peddled so fast in his life. He wasn't a regular cyclist, but he knew his way around a bike.

This time though, he was peddling a stationary bike, and he had to go as fast as humanly possible for 4,000 meters (2.48 miles).

And he wasn't alone.

He was in a room with other amateur cyclists. It was a mix of people. Some were old, some young.

He wasn't racing against them, though; he was racing against himself.

At the last quarter, his legs started giving out. His breathing was out of control.

Yet he remained focused and gave it his all. One final push. He gave it everything he had.

It felt like it took a thousand years.

Finally, the buzzer went off, and the instructor told him to get off the bike.

His legs felt numb from exhaustion. It took him several minutes to calm his breath to a point where he could ask the question.

"How did I do?"

The instructor replied, "We'll see, in the next round."

In the next round, John would race against himself.

The instructors recorded his first journey, and later he had to try and beat it.

John didn't know if he could, but as is his nature, he gave it 100%.

As he raced against himself, he felt the same exhaustion come over him. However, he knew if he simply stayed ahead of his own avatar from before, he'd win.

Once he finished, he was delighted to have beaten his previous personal best.

The other nine participants managed to do the same.

They all beat their previous records.

These nine men were part of a scientific study. The study ran over several trials and deliberately lied to the participants.

You see, the avatar was actually going faster than their previous ride.

Unknowingly, they were racing against a better version of themselves **and beat it**.

John's goal posts were moved. His task was immensely harder than he thought. Yet he crushed it.

After looking at the data, surprised at their findings, the scientists noted a very small increase in output from anaerobic sources. Nothing major.

In other words, John tapped just a small amount of additional energy to get a much greater outcome.

And most importantly, he beat himself.

In this chapter we're going to do the same. Together.

You see, with just a tiny bit more effort you can quickly see a 10%, 20%, or even 50% increase in income from your law office.

Remember, John the cyclist had one thing to focus on. Not three, not two, but one. He had to beat his own avatar.

That razor focus gave him the what he needed to succeed.

He didn't even worry about the other competitors.

I want you to do the same. Focus on getting this one thing done, and you'll discover a potential increase in income.

Let's dig in.

Every single month a few potential clients walk out of your law office because they cannot afford your fees.

Even though you promised them you will extend terms, they still won't budge. They just don't have the cash.

With financing, if we take industry averages into account, 30% of them will be able to get the money to afford your retainer.

Here's an example:

SMALL FIRM EXAMPLE:

Let's assume your **retainer is $6,500**, and **three potential clients** per month can't afford your fees.

The average increase in income: **$70,200 per year**.

MEDIUM FIRM EXAMPLE:

Let's assume your **retainer is $6,500**, and **fifteen potential clients** per month can't afford your fees.

The average increase in income: **$351,000 per year**.

LARGE FIRM EXAMPLE:

Let's assume your **retainer is $6,500**, and **seventy potential clients** per month can't afford your fees.

The average increase in income: **$1.63 million per year**.

Do see how easy it becomes to simply beat yourself by changing a simple thing in the way you do business?

You can do this yourself with a simple ROI calculator we programmed on EasyRetainer.legal/calculator.

Plug your numbers into the calculator, and it will spit out your potential increase in income.

You'd be surprised at how accurate it can be.

So how does it work?

How can an attorney offer financing to get clients to afford their fees, get paid up front, and increase income? **All without breaking bar rules?**

We touched upon this in the previous chapter; however, as an attorney I understand that you are naturally cautious and risk averse.

For this reason, a lot of attorneys dismiss this easy method of increasing their income out of hand.

Even though a few thousand attorneys are already using it to steal their clients, they refuse to accept that this is a viable option.

All because they haven't bothered to explore it further.

Just like the handlooms that were put out of business 200 years ago by John Bullough, these attorneys will get a rude wakeup call. And by then it is likely to be too late.

The trick is that you, the attorney, are not technically extending financing to the client.

The client applies for a personal loan from a financial institution. Their financial arrangement is with the bank, not the attorney or law office.

The client can technically spend the money on whatever they want. He can turn around and buy a vacation if he felt like it.

Let me give you an illustration.

John Doe walks into your office.

Before he even sits down with you, you've plugged his details into the financing system. It'll tell you, without pulling a credit report, whether or not John Doe qualifies for financing.

You'll even see what his monthly installments will be.

When John tells you that he cannot afford the retainer, you simply ask him, *"What can you afford on a monthly basis?"*

Since the client is in your office, he quite clearly need an attorney. There is no doubt in your mind that this guy needs your help.

So, if you present him with an affordable option, it becomes several magnitudes easier to get him as a client.

Below is an online review received by one of the attorneys we work with:

> *They were amazing right from the start. I met with him and explained my difficult situations with an ex who was so very unreasonable.*

> *I am a good father and simply wanted my fair time as is due me, but she had a much different vision for us even though she was on the road and not around for most of the child's lives while I raised them.*

> *Well Ryan was amazing through it all. Helped me lift that enormous stress that was sitting on my shoulders and got me basically everything I was asking for all while **allowing me time to pay**.*

> *Thank you, I will absolutely use you again in the future.*

Notice the part where the client expresses incredible thanks for giving him time to pay?

*"Helped me lift that enormous stress that was sitting on my shoulders and got me basically everything I was asking for all while **allowing me time to pay**."*

The problems your clients face are huge. For some of them, it will be the most difficult time of their lives.

What do you think happens when you offer to help with a simple and affordable way of paying?

Other attorneys are asking for big, upfront fees and unknowingly come across as greedy.

You, on the other hand, offering to solve their massive problems with easy, monthly installments with no upfront payments, will come across as the hero in their time of need.

I've seen this happen dozens and dozens of times.

Yet some attorneys are still hesitant.

And they will be left behind. It happens in every industry.

In the 1990s it was considered heresy to make beer from anything other than water, yeast, hops, and barley.

Yet, researching ancient brewing techniques led a man, named Sam Calagione, to make new and exciting beers.

His company is estimated to be worth $150–300 million.

By looking back at how other industries used financing in order to expand while helping their customers, the attorneys who take action will be the ones who prosper.

There is no need to be a pioneer or to pave the way. Simply do what other successful people have done in the past.

The waves are coming. You have to decide whether you are ready to take action or remain stationary.

Like Albert Einstein said, *"Life is like riding a bike. To keep your balance, you must keep moving."*

However, the benefits don't simply stop there. So far, we've only discussed the benefits of converting clients who can't afford your fees.

You also have a pool of clients every month you extend terms to.

This is a typical scenario I have come across.

Jane Doe comes into your office, and your retainer is $6,500.

She can't afford the full amount, so you get $3,000 up front. The rest is paid in monthly installments.

How many times have you done something like this?

Probably several times every single month.

The problem with this kind of "deal" is that 75% of people don't pay the full amount.

The attorney either reduces the fee, or the client simply stops paying.

This may or may not be a problem for you. Some law offices certainly have it worse than others.

Either way, you have no true recourse if someone doesn't pay you for the work you've done. You also don't get the money up front.

About 30–50% of your clients who you extend terms to will qualify for financing.

You'll get all of the cash up front, and you don't need to waste time chasing them down. This not only gives you a better cash flow position but also reduces the number of staff hours you spend following up on clients.

In other words, you'll get more money and reduce costs. An ideal situation for any business. All while making your clients happier with a new affordable option.

In the next chapter, we'll be using these happy clients to build you a massive 5-star reputation.

Effects of deception on exercise performance: implications for determinants of fatigue in humans. Stone MR, Thomas K, Wilkinson M, Jones AM, St Clair Gibson A, Thompson KG. Med Sci Sports Exerc. 2012 Mar;44(3):534-41. doi: 10.1249/MSS.0b013e318232cf77.

CHAPTER 4

How to Get A 5-Star Reputation with Clients Personally Recommending You to Complete Strangers

"Your brand or your name is simply your reputation, you have to fight in life to protect it as it means everything. Nothing is more important."

Richard Branson (1950), Billionaire founder of the Virgin Group

A FEW CHAPTERS ago I briefly mentioned two attorneys from Colorado, who were often mistaken for brothers they were so similar.

However, one was highly successful, and the other constantly flirted with being broke.

The successful attorney had a lot of free time and attracted high-paying clients.

The broke attorney worked ten to twelve hours per day with ungrateful clients who never seemed to have the cash to pay him.

After leaving law school and working for someone for a few years, the broke Colorado attorney set up his own firm.

It was just him and two other staffers.

He understood his area of law well.

He had helped several dozen clients at his previous firm and even scored some impressive victories against all odds.

He could be considered as one of the top in his field.

Yet every time a potential client walked into his office, he got frustrated and annoyed.

Why? Well, they always wanted a discount. They couldn't afford his fees. They were skeptical. They were shopping around for lawyers.

He blamed the potential clients. They simply "didn't get it."

The people in this little town outside of Denver simply weren't budging.

So he cut his prices and extended terms. He was working like a dog, day and night, simply to follow his so called "dream" of owning his own practice.

Had he known about financing, it would have eased his pain. However, he made one huge mistake in the way that he positioned himself.

Even if you don't have financing, this one change in his approach to running his law firm would have made all the difference. (I'll go into more detail in a minute).

Instead of fixing things where was located, he finally gave up decided that he needed to move to the city. That's where all of the rich people live, and he'll be able to charge higher prices.

However, his staffing costs were higher, his rent was higher, and he had to compete with ten times the number of attorneys.

Some of them were super attorneys, like his friend from law school.

He continued to struggle. Everything he tried seemed to fail.

The clients still demanded discounts. Some of them were still ungrateful. Nothing really changed except for the fact that now his costs had skyrocketed.

The other (successful) attorney seemingly took the same path.

He worked for another firm for a few years after law school and then proceeded to open his own small office.

And again, he struggled to attract good-paying clients.

However, instead of cutting his prices, he did something else.

He raised his prices. By a lot.

He then positioned himself as *The Divorce Attorney You Probably Can't Afford.*

He even had a price comparison chart showing how much more expensive he was.

He then printed case studies of his prior successful cases.

He even interviewed his happiest clients and displayed their wonderful words about him around the office.

As soon as people walked through that door, they knew that HE was the authority. Even though he was expensive, they believed that he could solve their problems.

In fact, they believed he could solve their problems BECAUSE he was expensive.

You see, what the successful attorney realized was that all of these people who "couldn't afford" his fees, were driving $30,000–50,000 cars, lived in their own homes, and lived decent lives.

Expense and price was never truly the REAL issue. It was only an excuse people were making. Sometimes people simply say they "can't afford it" to see if they can get favorable terms.

By increasing his fees, he almost automatically became the authority in his space.

The case studies and leaflets sealed the deal. People genuinely believed he was the best, because they were overwhelmed with *social proof.*

Social proof can come in the form of case studies, reviews, testimonials, etc.

The increased fees also meant he could deliver a better service to each client.

Not only did business improve, but so did the outcome of his cases.

So, instead of blaming the clients, he simply positioned himself differently.

People treated him with more respect, as they showed up on time and paid on time.

The broke attorney had contempt for his clients because he believed they were "cheap" and didn't appreciate his worth.

Let's take a look at how you can achieve what the successful attorney achieved, and avoid the path of the broke attorney.

Some attorneys shudder at the thought of increasing their fees. Don't worry. Even if you don't increase your fees, this will help you immensely.

Put that to one side.

First, let's focus on getting you a 5-star reputation so that you can be one of the most sought-after attorneys in your area, and perhaps even your entire state.

Imagine Jane Doe needs an attorney.

Her close friend, Gill, recommends *Attorney A*, who got her an amazing outcome.

Then Jane's brother recommends the same attorney because he had a great experience.

And finally, twenty other people personally recommend the same incredible attorney.

Then there is Attorney B. Nobody recommends him but himself.

Do you think Jane will use Attorney A or Attorney B?

Of course, she would use Attorney A. It is a no-brainer.

The successful attorney from Colorado copied this approach. Over the past ten years, it has become much easier to gain such a great reputation.

It is all because of this:

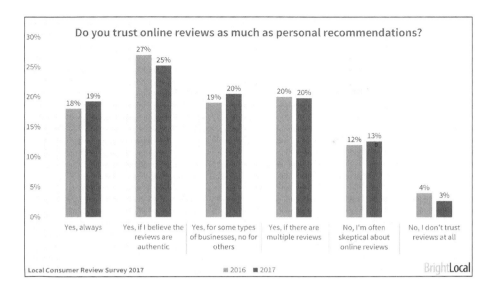

85% of consumers trust online reviews as much as personal recommendations.

Lots of 5-star reviews essentially is the same as your friends and family recommending you an attorney.

Just like Jane Doe's family and friends did in the hypothetical scenario above.

However, getting 5-star reviews often eludes many attorneys.

Only about 4% of all attorneys actively try to improve their reputation via reviews, even though it is by far the most effective and modern way to do so.

Relying on word of mouth is the equivalent of riding a horse and cart while everyone is driving a car.

You will fall behind, and quickly.

Not only is an online review the same as a personal recommendation in most cases, but it works for you, like a tiny little salesperson, 24 hours per day, 7 days per week.

You can have dozens, and even hundreds, of reviews working as little referral partners around the clock.

Word of mouth doesn't even come close.

So, you have a massive opportunity to get way ahead of the curve. By collecting reviews, the right way, you can join the top 4% of attorneys.

It is easier than you think with an effective reputation management system. We call it the Mass Referral System because of the number of referral quality leads it generates.

Picture this. You've finished fixing a client's legal problem, and you did a great job. The client is happy, and so are you.

Just before you guys shake hands on good terms, you do this one simple thing.

Ask him, *"Hey, before you go, do you mind writing a little review about your experience with me?"*

When he says, *"Yes, of course,"* simply hand him a tablet or your phone and ask him to rate you.

According to that same study I cited earlier, 68% of consumers left an online review if a business asked them.

The percentage is even higher when the process is easy and the client is happy.

Here's an example:

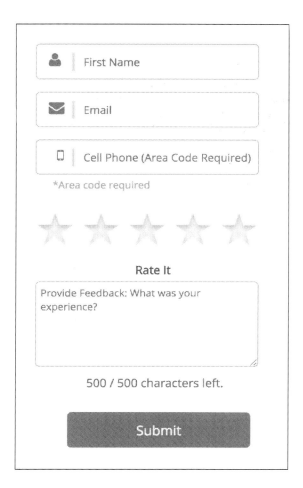

If the review is positive, the client will get an email asking him to share that review on Google, Facebook, Twitter, and other social platforms.

If the review is negative you get an email and a chance to address it.

This process is very important and can make or break a law firm. I cannot stress this enough. Businesses up and down the country are losing out on customers and clients.

Author and entrepreneur Kasio Martin wrote about her experience.

She wanted to use a local business. She Googled them and found they had a few good reviews.

Her experience with the business didn't go so well. She proceeded to write a bad review on five separate websites:

Insider Pages, City Search, Yahoo, Google Pages, and Yellow Pages.

According to Kasio, had she wanted to, she could have:

> Tagged their Facebook page and talked about my negative experience. I could have posted a negative review directly onto their neglected Facebook wall and (judging by their twice per year updates) they probably wouldn't notice for quite some time. What I am saying is that I can actually use their own Facebook page to divert their potential customers! Meanwhile I can also use 4Square to leave a helpful tip to do business elsewhere. Or even to advertise another business that treated me better.

The next time someone Googles that business, he would see Kasio's negative reviews five times before coming across one positive one.

And this brings me to my point. On average, a happy client will thank you and then go about their day.

An unhappy client will go out of their way to say bad things about you and your law firm.

One single unhappy person can turn away hundreds of new clients over the next few years.

So you need twenty to twenty-five happy clients for every one unhappy client.

It isn't fair. One angry client does not reflect the way that you do business. The super attorneys know this, and they use it to their advantage.

By controlling the review process, you can address the unhappy clients. You can finally balance the scale.

That's why it is so important to capture the negative review before it gets spread.

The Mass Referral System will notify you of the negative review so that you can contact the client.

This will reduce the chances of a bad reviewer getting out of control. Super attorneys don't like leaving things to chance.

The successful attorney from Colorado took action, and the broke attorney ignored it.

By simply using an easy review system and asking your happy clients for reviews, you could be pulling ahead of the pack in a major way.

Once you accumulate reviews, it becomes incredibly powerful.

Have a look at my company's review website:

That is almost 400 reviews, with an average rating of 4.97 out of 5.

As an attorney, when you are contemplating hiring a marketing company, would you look at these reviews?

The price of hiring an attorney is roughly the same as hiring a marketing company. If you see dozens, and in our case hundreds, of reviews, would that sway your decision?

My guess is that it'll play a big factor in whether or not you bite the bullet.

And it doesn't just end at our own review website. Have a look at what's on Google:

That is 67 reviews, with an average rating of 4.9 out of 5. These reviews work for me day and night to get new consulting clients. Each one is like a tiny little salesperson telling others how they should hire my team and me.

By taking your reputation seriously, it becomes difficult to say no to your services.

Charging higher prices becomes easier.

You can post these reviews on landing pages, social media, and your website.

You can print them out and have a review booklet that you hand to clients who walk into your law office.

When you get an objection from a potential client you can simply say, *"Don't take my word for it, simply read what other clients have experienced."*

It'll quickly become one of the most useful weapons in your arsenal. Other attorneys will look at you and wonder how on earth you are getting such high-paying clients all the time.

Here's a quick scenario that will happen week in and week out if you do this right.

Dave, a potential client, searches for an attorney in your area. Five or six results pop up.

You come out at the top with dozens of 5-star reviews.

Dave picks up the phone and gives you a call. When he comes into your office, he gets handed a little booklet with all of your reviews and case studies inside.

He's ready to hire you now before you've even spoken a word.

However, you are taking it one step further.

When you sit down and explain Dave's options to him, he asks about the price.

You explain that the best attorneys, who get the best results, are usually more expensive than other attorneys.

Dave agrees with you. He understands that you will cost more, and he believes that you are the best.

Then you hit him with an affordable financing option. It is well within his budget to pay monthly.

What are the chances of Dave becoming a client?

What do you think happens when you combine all of these elements?

He believes that you are the best, he knows he can afford you, and he knows that you will do a good job because you aren't cheap.

It is a powerful combination that'll catapult you to the top of the legal food chain.

Not only that, you'll save time by not needing to "convince" them of your worth. The reviews do that for you.

Instead of needing to be a salesman yourself, you'll have lots of tiny reviews working as salespeople for you 24 hours per day, 365 days per year.

You are more desirable and more affordable than your competition. You'll soon find yourself hoovering up more clients while getting paid more for your time.

All while your competitors are scratching their heads trying to figure stuff out.

While continuing my interview with Ken Hardison he had this to say about reviews for attorneys.

> "The last study I looked said 87% of people that go online to buy services or products, look at the reviews. And those Millennials are becoming a bigger market, and probably 95%, 98% of them look at reviews. So yeah, I think it's of utmost importance. You've got to have good reviews and that means you got to give a good service. And I've seen

some lawyers get some of the bad reviews, you know, and it hurts their business, there's no doubt about it.

There's some middle of the line lawyers doing it, but we preach that at PILMMA. We started preaching that a couple of years ago. And we teach them how to do it in an ethical matter. We've got some PILMAA members who have 300 or 400 reviews. Loads of them got 100 to 200 reviews. And they're seeing the benefit of it."

Do you see now how simple tweaks can make all the difference?

And how just doing a few things differently can turn you into a super attorney, with more time and money than regular attorneys?

Doing the things we've spoken about in this book so far will help you to quickly get more from existing leads and clients.

However, if you want to massively grow your firm, you'll need to expand on that. Use this initial success to catapult yourself onto a completely different a level.

This is a level that most attorneys can only dream of. Yet, I have seen average attorneys become powerhouses by simply applying the principles we're about to outline.

CHAPTER 5

How to Get More Clients on Autopilot

"Ordinary people think merely of spending time, great people think of using it."

Arthur Schopenhauer (1788–1860), German philosopher, Known for his 1818 work *The World as Will & Representation*

MARKITA ANDREWS JUMPED up with excitement.

She knew she was about to travel the world. She was thirteen years old, living with her single mother, a waitress in New York who had very little money to spare.

Yet that didn't faze her. In the magazine she was holding, there were clear instructions.

She started talking to her mom at over a hundred miles an hour about it. Her mom stopped her and said, *"I'll work hard to make enough money to send you to college. You'll go to college, and when you graduate, you'll make enough money to take you and me around the world. Okay?"*

"No, Mom!" she continued. *"Everything that I need to do is written in this magazine."*

Markita was reading her Girl Scout magazine. The Scout who sold the most cookies would win an all-expenses trip for two around the world.

She wouldn't have to wait until she got a job after college.

She simply had to sell more Girl Scout cookies than anyone had ever sold in the history of the Scouts.

The problem was that Markita wasn't smarter, more outgoing, or naturally talented than the average Scout. So, she did what she could with the little natural talent she had: Ask, ask, ask!

She would go to someone and ask them to buy cookies. If they didn't, she would ask them to think about it while she goes to the other potential buyers.

When she finished her rounds, she would go back to all of the potential buyers who agreed they would "think about it."

She would stand there, comfortable and confident, and ask them again.

In fact, Markita wasn't afraid to ask two, three, four, or even five times.

She kept reminding people that they expressed some kind of interest in her cookies. And as long as they still expressed an interest, she would continue to ask them.

In that first year, she sold 3,526 boxes of Girl Scout cookies and won a trip around the world for two.

Since then she has sold more than 42,000 boxes.

She's even co-authored a best-selling book called *How to Sell More Cookies, Condos, Cadillacs, Computers...and Everything Else.*

And her secret of "Ask, ask, ask!" is well known within the sales industry. Being persistent is one of the easiest ways to get new customers and clients.

For attorneys, who almost never apply this strategy, it is even more effective. And you can do it on autopilot without embarrassing yourself or annoying your potential clients.

How many times in your career have you had people leave your office, or hang up the phone, and you never hear from them again?

I assume, like with most attorneys, that number is uncomfortably high.

To overcome this, you first need to understand why this happens, because at first glance it doesn't make any sense.

If someone needs an attorney, or someone wants a box of cookies, why on earth do they procrastinate?

As an attorney, and you know this better than most people, getting your legal affairs in order shouldn't be put on a "waiting list." It should be done NOW.

So, when people visit your office or call you with a legal problem that needs solving, it is in their best interest to hire you right then and there.

Yet, in a lot of cases they don't.

Why?

Well, most people believe that procrastination stems from laziness or disorganization.

However, according to Pamela Wiegartz, PhD, that couldn't be further from the truth.

Procrastinators are often *"smart, capable, hardworking people..."*

Psychologists from all walks of life have tried to answer this question.

And by far the biggest reason why people don't solve big problems right away is **fear of failure**.

The second biggest reason why people don't get back to you is that **they forget**.

And luckily, there is a way to address both these things automatically. Once it is set up, you genuinely don't need to lift a finger.

Just like Markita, you're going to ask them to become a client more than once, while breaking down their fear of failure.

All you do is set up a system whereby you label or "tag" prospects.

If a prospect is on the fence, you can send them out a pre-determined series of emails and text messages. This works whether or not the prospect has called or have visited you in the office.

The sequence below has four touch points. You can easily have more. In some of our sequences, we have over thirty.

1. **Email** *(send immediately after initial contact)*: Thank them for coming in or calling. Then include reviews or case studies of previous happy clients.

2. **Text message** *(send immediately after initial contact)*: Thank them for considering your firm, and prompt them to store your phone number in their phone.

3. **Text message** *(send two days after initial contact)*: Check if they need any more help or information, and remind them to call you if they need anything.

4. **Email** *(send two to three days after initial contact)*:

Bring their attention to another case study or success story.

By simply following up with them, you've automatically done what nine out of every ten law offices never do.

Before I show you how to set this up so it happens automatically, let me give you a couple of templates you can use.

EMAIL 1

This email goes out immediately after contact, while you are still fresh in their mind. Studies have shown that you retain 80% more if you are reminded of that something on the same day.

The parts in **bold** need to be replaced with the appropriate words/phrases.

Subject line: One more thing…

Dear [FIRSTNAME],

*Thank you so much for **coming in [or calling]** to enquire about **[enquiry]**.*

*I just quickly wanted to let you know you are in good hands with **Mr/Mrs Attorney**.*

***She/he** has **x** years experience in handling cases like yours. For example, **Jane Doe** had this to say about **him/her**:*

"Here you would put an example review or testimonial. The more specific the review is about the situation the better the response rate will be."

Jane Doe

Even if the cases turn tricky, Mr/Mrs Attorney doesn't

back down. He/she had this happen a while ago, and the client said this about her/him.

"Here is another example review. The scenario above can be changed to whatever problem the attorney has overcome before."

John Doe

In fact, this law office has lots of reviews from clients who have had overwhelmingly positive experiences with us. Here are a few for you to read.

REVIEW 1

REVIEW 2

REVIEW 3

REVIEW 4

REVIEW 5

Please get in touch if you have any questions whatsoever by replying to this email. We're here to help you.

Kind regards,

[YourName]

END OF EMAIL 1

If you don't have enough reviews for this kind of campaign, then refer to the previous chapter.

You'll quickly discover that they will become the rocket fuel that propels your law office into new heights. They do all the heavy lifting for you.

TEXT MESSAGE 1

This message also goes out immediately, and it has two functions. The first is to get them to store your number in their phone. The second is to get them to read the email.

Your email has a 50/50 chance of being read, while your text message has a 90–95% chance of being read. You need to use that to your advantage.

*Hi [**FIRSTNAME**], this is [**yourname**] from **X Law Office**. Please save this number and call it if you ever have a legal problem. Make sure you save it.*

I also just sent you an email that has examples of people who were in your exact situation. Take a look at it now if you can.

All the best,

*[**yourname**]*

It is important that the text comes from an actual person, preferably the one they interacted with. Replace [yourname] with the name of that person.

This will boost response rates dramatically.

END OF TEXT MESSAGE 1

TEXT MESSAGE 2

This message goes out two to three days after the first text message and email. By now they have had time to think about it. Other alternatives might have crossed their path, but none of them are likely to make such good use of a follow up series.

This message will have a similar purpose to the first email—to remind them of you and get rid of their fear of failure.

Hi [FIRSTNAME],

*This is just a quick reminder. If you need any help, simply call us on this number. We've helped many people who needed an [**practice area**] attorney.*

*I am shortly going to drop you an email showing you how [**case study name**] got a great result from **his/her** case.*

All the best,

[yourname]

END OF TEXT MESSAGE 2

EMAIL 2

This email simply follows up from the text message you sent before. It should go out at the same time as the text message. Emails sometimes take longer to reach the potential client, so it is important to have it go out at the same time.

The case study you will put in this email can be long and detailed. Don't be afraid to add some of the difficulties you had with the case and how you overcame them.

People want to know that they are in good hands. They understand things don't always go according to plan and would like you to demonstrate the tricks you have up your sleeve to fix things.

It might just be another day in the office for you, but for them, any solution to a legal problem is close to a miracle. Non-attorneys are afraid of the complexity of the law. It is your job to put that fear at ease.

Hi *[FIRSTNAME]*,

*I hope all is well. A little while ago a **lady/man** came into our office with a very similar situation to you.*

*They needed **[explain what they needed from the attorney]**. It was important to them that it was handled quickly.*

Here's what happened:

[Explain what you did]

[Explain an obstacle you had to overcome]

[Explain the outcome]

***[Name of client]** was so happy they left us this review online:*

REVIEW

As you can tell, [attorney name] has a lot of experience in dealing with cases like yours.

Retaining him/her might be the best decision you could make.

Reply to this email so that we can talk more.

Kind regards,

[yourname]

END OF EMAIL 2

At this point, the client has heard from you four times from two different devices. This will help them to remember you when they decide to finally make a move.

Just because they procrastinate doesn't mean they don't need an attorney. They STILL need one. And your follow up communication with them will put you at the top of the list.

As I mentioned before, this is simply a basic follow up series. You can double, triple, or even quadruple the number of times you contact them.

For example, if you offer financing, you can have a couple of messages that talk about the affordability of your services.

You can even add in a case study about someone who couldn't afford your fees but used financing to retain you.

And best of all, this can be automated.

No matter how complicated the sequence gets, you can set up a pre-determined path that gets sent when a prospect gets "tagged."

Infusionsoft is one particular software we've used to automate this exact process. It allows you to be like Markita and ask, ask, ASK!

This was actually one of the first topics I discussed with Alexis Neely, who had this to say.

> "There was a woman who was in our Personal Family Lawyer program some years ago, and she went out and she got certified by this company called Infusionsoft, and now I have partnered with her. We've now built a custom Infusionsoft application, we call it Accelerator, for our member lawyers so that they can, in an automated and personalized way, remain in communication with the people that they have generated as leads, or who have become clients so they can build a real lifetime relationship with someone, so they can educate their community in the new way so that people don't fall through the cracks. And so, from that perspective, you know, technology is changing our industry in a huge way."

Unfortunately, I do not have the time to write a user manual on everything you can do with automation. And to be honest, you don't need to know how to do it. You simply need to know how to outsource it.

By using a service like Upwork, you can find experienced and competitive contract labor to help you automate your follow up process.

Now, let's take a look at what you could have achieved already in this book with the information you have been given.

You now know that there are only two ways to grow your law firm. You understand that you need to focus on those two things and those two things only.

So far, we've only discussed ways to increase your income from your existing leads and clients.

You can use financing to become more affordable to your clients while getting your retainer up front and in full.

You can show prospects dozens and dozens of reviews and case studies. You are collecting them week in, week out. Your gold-star reputation keeps growing, and you'll find that you become more respected while attracting higher paying clients.

You can use a follow up series for those who fall through the cracks to bring them back. You can lay their fears to rest and constantly remind them that you are the authority in the space.

Are you starting to see how many small tweaks to your law firm can make a huge difference? The super attorneys who make use of these strategies and techniques don't work any harder than you do. In fact, they simply work smarter. Joining them is easy.

Simply do what Markita did and start implementing some of these ideas.

CHAPTER 6

Phone Secrets: Get Your Staff to Utter These Words on the Phone to Get More Clients

"If you just communicate you can get by. But if you communicate skillfully you can create miracles."

Emanuel James "Jim" Rohn (1930–2009), American entrepreneur, author, and motivational speaker

A FEW MONTHS ago, I had an attorney call me up—and she was furious.

I recognized the number. It was a client of ours.

At first, I thought she was joking. I thought she was about to tell me that she could not believe how much her law firm has grown in just thirty short days.

I wish.

She called to yell at me. And when I say "yell," I mean it.

She said, *"You don't know what you are doing, and this whole thing was a waste of time and money."*

I was shocked.

I said, *"Hold on a minute; I don't understand. You've had twenty-eight inbound calls from people who are actively looking for a lawyer like you, in just the last thirty days."*

She quickly cut me off, *"They're all useless. None of them were serious prospects."*

I told her that I would look into it.

At first I was perplexed. I had successfully tripled an attorney's business (who was in the same area of law) just the month before.

How could it be so different?

So I did some digging, and what I found shocked me.

Luckily, we recorded every inbound call.

This helps us to track whether or not the advertising works. It is also a great exercise to help improve your staff (more about that in a minute).

It also helps us to pinpoint what the quality of the prospects is. Some campaigns yield better customers than others.

This is an example of one client's campaign (not the one I am referring to now):

So I started listening to the very first call.

In this case, we could see that a prospect went to Google and typed in *"divorce lawyer quick."*

Based on what she was searching, one would assume she needed a divorce attorney, and she needed one quickly.

As expected, the prospect saw our attorney's ad and dialed the number on the landing page.

Here's a quick transcript from that call.

Ring ring... ring ring...

Office: *"Hi"*

Prospect: *"Hello?" [pause]*

Office: *"What do you want?" [chewing something]*

Prospect: *"I wanna talk to a divorce person... to help with my-ah-husband."*

Office: *"OK, can you call back later? I'm on lunch."*

Prospect: *"Alright..."*

Phone hangs up

That was the very first conversation. It lasted about twenty seconds.

I couldn't believe it.

She had to realize that she was not the only attorney around. That prospect is going straight to another Google search and finding a different attorney. She just handed her competition a big wad of cash.

I then went ahead and listened to another call.

Ring ring... ring ring...

Office: *"Yeah...?"*

Prospect: *"Hi, is this err... the law office? I want to talk about my husband." [pause]*

Office: *"Yeah, this is a law office."*

Prospect: *"..." [silence]*

Office: *"OK, well what do you want?"*

Prospect: *"Alright..."*

Office: *"Do you know what you want or do you want to call back later?" [interrupts them]*

Prospect: *"I just have a question..."*

Office: *"OK, well what is it?" [cuts them off again]*

Prospect: *"How much does it cost to get a divorce?"*

Office: *"Err… well I've seen it as high as $7,500 before, but it isn't always the same. Wait… yeah… a lot of times it is around $7,500, but the price starts at $2,500. But err… yeah $7,500 like sometimes even more like $10,000."*

Prospect: *"Wow that's a lot more than I err… thought."*

Office: *"Yeah I've seen it at $7,500 a lot so…"*

Prospect: *"OK, thank you I'll think about it."*

Phone hangs up

The tone of voice, the interruptions, and the contempt for the prospect was clear as day.

Again, I was shocked. It was as if this law office was irritated that people were inquiring about hiring them.

Each one of those two conversations could have resulted in multiple thousands of dollars for the attorney.

Any single one of those cases could have paid for one to two month's worth of advertising.

I'll give you an exact script of what your staff should be saying in a minute.

And don't worry—it is dead simple. Anyone could do this.

I went through all twenty-eight calls. There were eight people who actually ASKED to hire the attorney, and somehow the person on the phone managed to repel them.

Another eleven people could have been booked in for one-on-one appointments.

Four more could have been persuaded if the person on the phone was just a little persistent.

The remaining five were timewasters. So out of twenty-eight

calls, you could imagine that they'd get at least five to ten cases out of it.

That's at least $15,000 worth of business right there, and it might even have been $50,000.

A few months before starting this book, a client of mine got a case from his online advertising that netted him $89,000.

If his staff didn't answer the phone correctly, that case could have gone to his competitor. And since we're talking about inbound calls, the prospects on the phone are desperate for you to help them. All you need to do is nudge them in the right direction.

Now let us have a look at an actual transcript from one of our more successful attorneys. Of course, all of the names have been removed for privacy reasons.

Ring ring…

Office: *"[Attorney name] Law Office, this is [name]. How can I help you?"*

Prospect: *"Oh, hi there. I was wondering if you could give me some advice?"*

Office: *"Of course! What would you like advice on?"*

Prospect: *"I want to… err… divorce my… err… husband."*

Office: *"OK, well you've come to the right place. We'll take really good care of you. May I take your name?"*

Prospect: *"[Name]"*

Office: *"OK, [Prospect name], how about I schedule you a free one-on-one appointment with our attorney, Mrs. [Attorney name]. She'll be able to answer all of your questions in detail.*

She's incredibly good at divorce cases. Do you have time to come in on Tuesday?"

Prospect: *"Err… yeah I can't make Tuesday; I can make Thursday though."*

Office: *"Sure thing, would 10:00 a.m. work for you?"*

Prospect: *"Yes, 10:00 a.m. is fine."*

Office: *"Perfect, she'll see you on Thursday at 10:00 a.m. here at our office. The address is [Address]. I'll send you an email and a text message with the information. What's your cell number?"*

Prospect: *"[Cell number]"*

Office: *"OK, and your email address?"*

Prospect: *"[Email address]"*

Office: *"Alright, you are all set, [Prospect name]. Don't forget that it is very important to get advice as quickly as you can, because divorce cases reward those who are the best prepared."*

Prospect: *"Oh thank you so much. I won't forget that [laugh]. I see you on Thursday."*

Office: *"Thank you! Have a wonderful day."*

Phone hangs up

Can you see the difference?

A simple divorce case can bring in about $2,500 in quick cash.

Some of the more complicated cases can bring in $10,000, $30,000, and even $1 million (on rare occasions).

So by messing up just one phone call, you could be missing out on tens of thousands of dollars.

You are basically giving that money away to your competitors.

The second transcript shows how a pro does it.

And it isn't difficult.

Anyone can be taught to close on the phone like that with simple training. I'll give you the exact blueprint for closing sales in a minute.

First, let me give you an exact breakdown of what is going through your prospects' minds when they are calling you. Knowing this is the key to getting more clients from your existing leads.

Your potential clients are in pain.

So much so that they decided to go over to Google to search for an attorney.

That might not seem like a big deal, but trust me, it is.

Nobody looks for a lawyer until they absolutely HAVE TO.

It isn't like going out to dinner. They understand that the process is complex, they believe it is expensive, and they feel like it will be difficult. The longer they can postpone it, the longer they can avoid the pain.

However, they have a huge problem to solve, and they are hoping to find someone to solve it for them.

Finally, they pluck up the courage and do a Google search.

They find you and your landing page or website.

Now they have to make a decision.

Do they postpone it by one more day, or do they finally take action?

A recent Harvard Study showed how the majority of humans

always postpone difficult decisions if they can. And countless other studies have proven the same.

However, the prospects manage to fight their own human nature to seek help with their problem.

So they pick up the phone to call you.

Now imagine someone who doesn't care answers the phone. The person who answers the phone deals with people like this every single day. To him it is boring and monotonous.

Not to your prospects. It is the exact opposite. In some cases, they would never deal with a situation like this.

This one problem that your prospects are facing is the BIGGEST thing in their lives right now.

And the person on the other side of the phone (at your firm) could be making your prospects feel awful without even knowing it. Even if they are polite, the prospects are quick to find reasons not to hire you.

They are constantly second guessing everything. They are evaluating your every word and certain things will trigger them to leave without hiring you.

Most people don't tend to call back once they have decided against hiring you.

Most people will go somewhere else where they feel assured and wanted. Great attorneys are aware of this. Zaid Abdullah had this to say on the matter.

> *"If you've gotten 100 phone calls but you've only retained one client. Well, then maybe it's something in my office that's not working. And when you can go ahead and pinpoint every point of the client acquisition process, and you can fine tune every part of it, your conversion is going to go through the roof, and in turn, your rate of return is going to go through the roof."*

The sad truth is most law offices in America have good quality staff. They are polite and professional. Yet, they still do and say things that turn people away. It isn't your fault or your staff. There is no way to know unless you have recorded and studied hundreds of calls.

That's what we did.

My team and I made a list of calls.

There were two columns. One was a successful call where the prospect became a client.

The other column was a failed call, where the prospect did not become a client.

Out of the forty-two law firms, we found four who had a much higher success rate than the others.

In fact, they would get three to four times the number of clients.

After careful study, we found that there is a pattern, a simple blueprint for answering the phone, that drastically improves the success rate.

Without changing anything in your firm, without spending any more money on marketing, and without needing to spend weeks training your staff, you could see a vast improvement by simply following this simple blueprint.

STEP #1: MAKE THEM FEEL LIKE THEY MADE THE RIGHT DECISION

Remember, these prospects feel like they have a huge problem, bigger than most things in their lives, and they constantly second guess their decisions.

So the very first thing you need to do is make them feel like they made the right decision. This simple act will boost their confidence level in you.

You achieve that by doing the following:

1. Answer the phone professionally: *"[Attorney name] Law Office, this is [name]. How can I help you?"*

2. They will tell you what they want.

3. Let them know they are in the right place: *"OK, well you've come to the right place. We'll take really good care of you. May I take your name?"*

I told you it was simple. You do not have to be a genius salesperson to do this.

STEP #2: PROVE THAT YOU'LL TAKE CARE OF THEM

Try and get them to commit to a time to come in for a face-to-face. It'll make them feel important, AND it makes the sale easier.

Your office is the expert, the authority, the one thing that is going to solve their problem. You need to guide them; don't let them guide you.

You have to position it correctly though. Give them a free consultation and reinforce how good the attorney is at dealing with their particular situation.

OK [prospect name]. How about I schedule you a free one-on-one appointment with our attorney Mrs. [Attorney Name]. She'll be able to answer all of your questions in detail. She's incredibly good at divorce cases. Do you have time to come in on Tuesday?

Did you notice how simple and direct it is?

Your staff took control of the situation and suggested a day for the prospect to come in.

Do not ask them if they would like to come to talk to the attorney, simply assume that they do. Remember, your office, not the prospect is the authority and the expert. They want you to lead them and guide them.

STEP #3: BE CLEAR ON THE BENEFITS OF A ONE-ON-ONE APPOINTMENT

A lot of times, prospects are just going to want advice over the phone. And that's fine.

However, you can always give them a nudge to come in and become a client—especially if it is the secretary answering the phone.

Do that by emphasizing the benefits of a one-on-one appointment and the consequences of NOT hiring you.

> *The best thing would really be for you to talk to the attorney face-to-face, because the quicker you get advice the more prepared you will be. The more prepared you are, the better the outcome for you.*

> *You could quickly gain the upper hand here if you choose to. Plus, the consultation is free. You literally have nothing to lose. I see that [attorney name] has availability on [day] at [time]. Shall I book you in for that time?*

That can literally work for almost any kind of law.

Here's an example of a DUI case:

> *Remember I said that you are in good hands here? Well, [attorney name] has done hundreds of these cases, and*

his clients who get the best outcome are the ones that act quickly.

Only then is it possible to gain the upper hand and perhaps get you off the charges completely. There are no guarantees, but the quicker you move, the easier it is. Can I book you in for [day] at [give time]?

Notice how these simple statements take control of the conversation.

And if the prospect says, "No," after this point, then let them go. They weren't ready to hire an attorney yet.

STEP #4: HANDLING QUESTIONS ABOUT PRICE

By now you have them hooked. However, some people still want to know about the huge price tag.

Luckily, movies and TV series have already portrayed the best lawyers to be the expensive ones.

This gives you a decided advantage over other professions.

Whatever you say, remember to start with this:

It really depends on how big the caseload is. I've done cases that were $100,000 and others that were $1,000 [mention lowest price last]. The biggest thing that determines the case load is how quickly you tackle the problem.

This creates urgency. Now they HAVE to come in as quickly as possible because it'll save them money.

If you offer financing, this question becomes even easier to answer.

And sir, we have financing options available so you could be looking at small monthly payments. We'll be able to determine everything if you come in and talk to us.

Don't forget to ask them for the appointment again.

> *So, Mr. [prospect surname], how about we do this. I'll book you in for [day] at [time], and the attorney will be able to explain everything to you.*
>
> *Like I said before, it doesn't cost you anything. Do you have availability at that time?*

Notice how hard it is to fight the logic? By following this meticulously you'd be able to fill up the appointment book with new cases pretty easily.

These are only examples. Your staff will need to find their own voice when it comes to this. Understanding the concepts behind these steps is almost more important than the scripts I am giving you.

The first time I consulted with a law firm about handling their inbound calls, I used a simple method to train their staff.

First, I took all of the calls and transcribed them.

I took out the names of the clients and the staff who answered the calls.

I then compared each call next to a checklist.

- Did the staff make the client feel like he was taken care of?

- Was the staff clear on the benefits of a one-on-one appointment?

- Did the staff take control of the conversation?

- Did the staff handle questions and objections by pushing the one-on-one consult?

• Was the staff professional and polite?

Each call would get a rating, and we'd simply have a quick recap on what the staff should have said.

Since everything is anonymous, the staff aren't embarrassed about getting something wrong.

These exercises have worked miracles in once struggling law firms. Firms that are already doing pretty well seem to soar to the heavens after these simple changes are made to the way to talk to prospects.

Every single one of the things we've discussed so far in this book could help to grow your law firm.

So far, we have covered:

1. Becoming more affordable via financing.

2. Getting more clients by using case studies and reviews.

3. Using a follow up series to remind clients to come back to you.

4. Using a simple script to get more clients who have called in.

If each of these four things improve your results by just 20%, you would have doubled your law firm's business.

Here's a quick illustration.

Let's say you usually get twenty clients per year.

After becoming more affordable via financing, you get a 20% increase in clients saying, "Yes."

This brings your total to 24 clients per year.

Then, by using case studies and reviews, you increase the clients who say, "Yes," by another 20%.

This gives you 28.8 clients per year.

The same happens by using the follow up series, and the number of clients you get increases to 34.6 per year.

Once you implement the phone scripts discussed in this chapter, the last 20% increase takes you to just over 40 clients per year.

This is, of course, just a hypothetical scenario.

It doesn't tend to work out this smoothly in real life.

Each law firm is at slightly different points on the scale.

However, hopefully this has demonstrated how you can make a few little tweaks to the way your firm operates to see huge growth.

By simply improving each stage of the client acquisition process, you suddenly find yourself with more clients, more cash, and a better running law firm. All without spending another dime on marketing and advertising.

Every ounce of growth has come from the potential you already had locked up in your firm.

All you need to do is use the keys I have given you to unlock those doors.

Unlocking these doors will become essential as the waves of change come crashing into the legal industry, sweeping away everyone who is unprepared to move with the times.

The steps are simple, yet they are vital.

CHAPTER 7

Use the Super Attorney's "Major Cash Cheat Sheet" for Instant Growth

"There is no short cut to achievement.
Life requires thorough preparation—
veneer isn't worth anything."

George Washington Carver (1860s–1943),
American botanist and inventor

MAJOR PLOYER P. HILL sat in the cockpit. As a pilot for the U.S. Army Air Corps, he was one of the best.

He was just waiting for the "OK" from command.

It was 1935 and the U.S. military was just about to acquire one of the deadliest planes in history.

It would come to be known as "The Flying Fortress."

At the time, it was by far the most sophisticated airplane that was ready to go into production.

Boeing spared zero expense at putting an elaborate show on for the military commanders.

This deal would propel them into the billion-dollar corporation that came to dominate the aviation industry over the next seventy-five years.

They were all watching in anticipation at Wright Field in Dayton, Ohio.

The pilot, Major Hill, finally got the "OK." He was excited. He had never flown a plane that was this well put together.

The takeoff was perfect. It was smooth, stable, and achieved perfect lift.

Everyone looked on with excitement and pride. The smiling faces of the commanders soon turn to faces of horror.

Within seconds of achieving the perfect takeoff, the plane stalled and crashed into the field.

Crash of Model 299 on October 30, 1935

Major Ployer Hill did not survive.

Embarrassed and confused, the Boeing bosses immediately started an investigation.

They found something very odd. In actuality, what puzzled them most was the absence of anything odd.

There seemed to be nothing wrong with the plane. It was in perfect condition.

There were no mechanical failures whatsoever. Everyone was perplexed.

They investigated further, double-checked, and triple-checked everything. Nothing.

Then they started taking eyewitness accounts, including that of the surviving co-pilot, and what they found was astonishing.

The flight crew had simply forgot to release the flight control gust locks. In other words, the plane was still in park mode. This caused it to nosedive soon after takeoff.

Shortly afterwards, Boeing introduced a mandatory checklist.

Eventually, they were able to sell the Model 299, and it flew for years without incident.

Today, you can't take off or land in a commercial airplane without a mandatory checklist being used by your pilots.

It doesn't stop there; from the creation of each plane, to maintenance checks, to the flight attendants who assist with your in-flight service, checklists are mandatory throughout the airline industry.

The checklists keep improving. The year 2017 was the safest on record. Some pilots refer to the checklist as their "cheat sheet" to saving human lives.

Businesses up and down America who use these checklists

or "cheat sheets" tend to grow faster, make less mistakes, and serve their customers better. That's why I named it the "Major Cash Cheat Sheet," after pilot Major Hill.

For example, a study in 2009 showed that introducing a checklist in surgery reduced deaths by half, and complications fell by more than a third.

Even though the surgeons and teams had experience and knew what they were doing, they still benefited from a cheat sheet.

Can you imagine how much someone who doesn't have experience could benefit from a cheat sheet? The potential for a shortcut to success is immense.

The same is true for you and your staff. Instead of maximizing safety, you're going to maximize income and client satisfaction.

By having a clear and dedicated cheat sheet, you'll be performing all the tasks you need in order to keep increasing the cash coming into your firm. The more cash you have, the better you can serve your clients.

Luckily, growth checklists for attorneys are simple. It isn't anything like flying an airplane or fixing someone's spine.

After working with countless attorneys to grow their law firms, we have certain cheat sheets that work better than others.

Each firm will slightly tweak the cheat sheet as it goes along to suit its workflow.

The following is an example of an Easy Retainer® Cheat Sheet:

CHEAT SHEET: Easy Retainer* (Growth via Financing)		
This process has been designed to make it as seamless as possible for the client. All the client has to do is say yes or no once the meeting with the attorney is finished.		
1.	Get primary client information	This is done on the phone. E.g. Name, address, phone number, email, etc.
2.	Get secondary client information	This is done in person. The secondary information will be more in depth and will allow you to check if the client will be able to qualify for financing. This can be done on a tablet or a physical form.
3.	Submit information to check eligibility	This happens before the attorney even sees the client for the initial consultation. The client may not even know that. IMPORTANT: Checking the client's eligibility does NOT pull a credit report or affect the client's credit in any way.
4.	Send financing result to attorney	Before the attorney even speaks to the client, the attorney will know whether or not the client qualifies for the basic retainer.
5.	Attorney meets with client	Once all of the legal options have been explained to the client, you can offer the option of financing, knowing whether or not the client will qualify.
6.	Offer financing options	Ask the client whether he would like to see the repayment options for financing the retainer. It is important to offer this to ALL clients who qualify, regardless whether or not they can pay up front. Some might prefer the monthly payments and will be happier because of it.
7.	Apply for financing	Once the client has confirmed he would like to go for financing, either let him submit the form on a tablet, or get him to do it on your computer. You already have all the information ready, so this process is quick.

For example, you may choose to use Google Sheets to collect their answers or use a CRM to automatically tag them in each process. Or perhaps you'll simply keep them on paper.

The aerospace industry still updates their lists so why shouldn't you?

In this case it is important to use it and tick off the process as the clients go through it.

Especially with financing. Once you get in a habit of offering it, you'll see how seamless it becomes. Clients love it, you get more cash up front, and it removes delinquencies.

All because of a simple one-page cheat sheet. It is so effective I would recommend this to be the very first growth strategy you implement in your firm. The second thing you should implement are reviews.

As with financing, you need to weave reviews into the very fabric of how you do business. Nothing turns you into more of an authority in your business than a bunch of 5-star online reviews. The cheat sheet will help with that.

There was one law firm, out of Connecticut, who went from almost giving up, to thriving, because they used it. As with any growth tool, the Mass Referral Reviews System is useless without proper implementation.

On the flipside, once you start doing it regularly you'll find yourself getting addicted to it. There is no better feeling, in the business world, than seeing clients praise your services.

Work is a big part of life, and when people appreciate it so much they share it with the world, there is a deep satisfaction that comes with that.

On the following page you will find the reviews cheat sheet. Once you have your mini review website set up with everything in place, start using it like your livelihood depends on it. With the coming waves of change, it just might.

CHEAT SHEET: Mass Referral System (Growth via Reviews)

This process has been designed to get the maximum number of reviews online so that you can use them to grow your law firm.

1.	Have tablet or laptop ready in the office	Always be prepared in the office to take a review. The process is quick, and the review page should always be kept open.
2.	After the initial free consultation	Try and get the first review after the initial free consultation. A lot of prospects will feel like a weight has been lifted, because the options in their case have been made clear.
3.	Get the client to write the review	If you feel the client has had a positive experience, ask them to write a review. You can even collect it on physical paper forms, and then type it up later. Remember to add their email address so they can be prompted to share their positive review online.
4.	After services have been rendered	Once you have finished with a client and they are happy with your services, ask them for another review. Getting more than one review from a single client is common, especially since the first and last review will be weeks/months apart.
5.	Write down short description of case	Try and match the review with specific cases. This will allow you to create specific case studies down the line that make it easier to close future clients.
6.	Get professional review booklet printed	Once you have collected lots of reviews, get a small booklet printed called Client Results. Here you can put an imagine of the online review with the five stars on the page, and add the short description of the case and why the client was so happy. Put this booklet in your waiting room, your office, and your reception desk.
7.	Use the booklet to get more clients	During your initial consultations with prospects, you can refer to specific cases, that are relevant to them, and explain what happened. Make sure they understand that not all cases are the same, but these are outcomes that have happened in the past.

When I consult with law offices, I will always have these cheat sheets handy. One of the tasks will be for us to go through each one. The staff, or the attorney, have to give me examples of how they have used it.

We'll comb through all of their experiences.

What went well? What went bad? What didn't make sense?

This helps to reinforce the existing sheet as well as adding to it. At the end of the initial consulting period of a few weeks, the office is likely to see consistent growth and smooth implementation. Then we move onto the next big growth strategy.

There is always a steady and consistent movement towards growth. The ONLY thing that will prevent the firm from growing is if it does not implement or act on the tasks at hand. They are simple, yet some law offices are not putting in the necessary minimal effort to get it done.

John Bullough had a very simple solution when it came to the handloom. Out of the 200,000 employed in northern England, he wasn't the only one who knew about the difficulties and limitations of the machine.

However, he was the only one who took the simple steps to improve how it works. He got handsomely rewarded while others lost their jobs.

As an attorney, it is even easier. You don't have to reinvent the wheel and try untested strategies. You simply have to implement what is tried and tested already.

You know this stuff works. You simply need to mobilize yourself, and your staff, to get it done.

Here's one way you can make sure your cheat sheet gets implemented.

Split the sheet into two categories:

- One-off tasks
- Ongoing tasks

The one-off tasks are pretty self-explanatory. You do them once, and you don't have to do it again. For example, getting a cheap tablet in order to collect reviews.

The ongoing tasks need to be broken up into daily, weekly, monthly, or client tasks.

A client tasks refers to a task which needs to be completed once a client is involved. It doesn't have a specific time associated with it.

An example of a daily task might be to type up reviews written on paper by the client. Another task may be to update the review booklet and get more printed. Depending on how many reviews you get, you might want to do it only once every quarter and not every month.

Assign each task to a specific member of the staff. You may even have one person doing all of them.

I once worked with an attorney who printed each staff member's tasks on small cards that they can carry around with them. This worked very well, especially in the beginning when everything was new.

The staff would constantly consult their little cards and write notes on them. We'd go around the room and review all of the tasks from the week using those little cards.

Hopefully you are starting to see the value of cheat sheets that can help your law firm to grow. Even the best pilots and surgeons in the world use their own cheat sheets to get the best results.

We have cheat sheets for every single growth strategy, and we use them with all of our clients. They are invaluable when trying to implement.

Don't forget, procrastination doesn't only affect your prospects; it may affect you and your staff as well.

CHAPTER 8

Use the "Problem First" Approach to Quickly Get New Clients

"Successful people are always looking for opportunities to help others. Unsuccessful people are always asking, 'What's in it for me?'"

Brian Tracy (1944), Canadian-American motivational public speaker and self-development author

DEMOSTHENES, A YOUNG Athenian boy, couldn't speak well. He stuttered, struggled to form sentences, and, as a consequence, suffered in his early years.

He still felt fortunate because his father was a wealthy sword maker. However, it was short lived. At the age of seven, he was orphaned.

His father had prepared for this day and left him an inheritance. In today's money, it would be about $11 million.

However, his guardians didn't look after his inheritance like they should have. They completely mishandled it and left him with a fraction of what he was due.

Determined to take them to court, he sought out the help of others who could speak well and understood the law. However, in ancient Greece, it was illegal to pay someone to help you with your case. So, he decided to do it himself.

What happened next was nothing short of remarkable. Demosthenes built an underground study where he could learn in peace and practice speaking.

He constantly spoke with pebbles in his mouth, rehearsed in front of mirrors, and would repeat sentences while out of breath or running. He would also obsessively read about speeches given by great public speakers. To improve his voice, he would travel to the seaside and speak above the roar of the ocean.

As soon as Demosthenes came of age in 366 BC, he took his guardians to court. His three guardians felt confident that he wouldn't be able to string together a single coherent sentence. Yet when the time came, he was flawless.

He went through five separate trials and was rewarded an additional ten talents, which was about the 70% of his inheritance that was missing.

His newfound abilities didn't go unnoticed. Rich and powerful men will flout the rules of hiring an advocate.

Demosthenes found himself representing clients and winning cases. He seems to have been able to manage any kind of case, adapting his skills to almost any client.

He quickly filled a huge void. At times, the cases were very complicated and included a lot of plaintiffs. He helped to solve problems people found impossible to solve themselves.

Now he is widely considered to be one of the first recorded attorneys by today's definition.

Before he stepped into public office, he earned his entire living by solving people's legal problems.

When he spoke, he didn't refer to himself or his character. He spoke about people's problems and appealed to their need to have their problems solved. Whether in court or in public, he would win people's approval.

And that is exactly what attorneys in America are not doing. The super attorneys who are doing this are tapping into an unlimited source of new clients who are willing to pay premium prices.

It was this realization that propelled me into helping law firms grow.

Several years ago, I ran a successful business generating leads.

One day the phone rang.

"As many leads as you can possibly deliver..."

I replied, *"Are you sure? Will you be able to handle it?"*

"Yes, bring it on..."

And so I did. I flipped the switch to "On." My team jumped into action and started on a campaign with no limits.

Within four days, we were generating between 2,000 and 10,000 leads per day. A couple of years later, it was the biggest online university in the country. It turns out they really *could* handle it.

A short while afterwards, an attorney called me.

I'm not sure if, as an attorney, you know how heart-stopping it can be when you call someone out of the blue.

So, I sat there holding my breath. Wondering if I'm about to get screwed in some way by some unknown entity.

As soon as the attorney started talking, I sighed with relief.

All he wanted was a steady stream of inbound calls requesting his services. In other words, I was asked if I could generate leads for a local law office.

I had never generated a single lead for an attorney before. So, I suggested we set up a test.

After all, I could simply take what I learned from the 500,000 leads I just generated for my biggest client.

I performed 5,000 tests, ran over 100,000 ads, and was pushing 10,000–20,000 visitors per day to their lead generation pages.

I knew what worked, but would it be the same for lawyers?

It turns out law offices are very different from other businesses.

I ran the first test for the attorney, and it fell flat. After two days—nothing. Not a single lead.

However, this simple failure would reveal one of the biggest secrets when it comes to growing a law firm, something Demosthenes unknowingly championed over two millennia ago.

I decided to figure out what the problem was by surveying the visitors with a special piece of software.

I asked them two simple questions:

> 1. What area of law are you looking to inquire about?

> 2. What problem do you want to solve?

And something odd happened. At first glance, I thought the survey had failed. Most people skipped the first question and only answered the second question.

I was about to call my colleague to ask him to see how quickly we could set up another survey, when something caught my eye.

There was something incredibly interesting about the answers to the second question. People would write these huge paragraphs and go into incredible detail about the problem they want solved.

I couldn't figure out why. My first thought was that people believed the attorney got their answers. Perhaps they believed the attorney would respond.

However, upon further inspection, that was impossible. The wording was perfectly clear. They even had to tick a box acknowledging they knew an attorney wouldn't get back to them.

I spent the whole day thinking about it. I couldn't shake the feeling that we did something wrong.

That night I sat down to watch a baseball rerun. As the commercials started, my hand stood still over the fast-forward button.

There was a commercial for a car. I believe it was a Ford. Instead of hitting the fast-forward button, I thought I would pay attention. For whatever reason, I decided to sit there and watch a commercial.

It was pretty good. I was engaged, and I felt uplifted. I could actually see myself in that Ford.

The next commercial was completely different. I felt the exact opposite.

It was some tablet or medicine that helped with some kind of disease. They showed people suffering and then demonstrated how it can help you.

It was such a contrast to the first Ford commercial that I immediately started comparing them.

And that's when it hit me like a ton of bricks.

It turns out the attorney market is very different to other markets. That is why so many attorneys fail at advertising their services.

And the reason is simple. Nobody has a **desire** to hire an attorney.

People have a desire for a flat screen TV, morning coffee, and a new car. That Ford commercial appealed to my desires for something that'll elevate my status among my peers.

Hiring an attorney is different.

Take the commercial selling medicine, for instance. Nobody has a desire to contract a disease that requires them to fork out cash to make them better.

Just like nobody has the desire to have a legal problem so large they need to hire an attorney.

Attorneys don't fulfil desires like other products and businesses do.

You are in the business of *solving problems*. Very real and very serious problems.

So your marketing and advertising has to be different. In most cases, it has to be drastically different.

After realizing this, I felt excited. Everything made sense. The next morning, I instructed my team to make a few tweaks to the advertising campaign.

What happened next shocked me and my new attorney friend.

Five new clients signed up in the next seven days, netting him an additional $35,000 in new business.

All of a sudden, I was hailed a "genius" by an attorney. To this day, I am not sure if I explained to him that I was an "accidental genius."

And the process was simple.

Focus solely on solving a single problem, and make sure the prospects knew you understood it inside and out.

It is funny how history repeats itself over and over.

Demosthenes understood how to solve people's problems. He was incredible at communicating his ability to do so, and he used it to turn himself into one of the most famous orators and politicians of Ancient Greece.

Commercials for medicine are good at exactly the same thing.

Now we simply needed to apply that same principle to modern day law offices.

The difference in results is startling.

Imagine there are two lawyers, both of whom do exactly the same thing. Both of them are equally qualified to offer the same service and are good at what they do.

So, both of them start an advertising campaign using Google.

Lawyer #1 gets fifty clicks from Google.

Lawyer #2 gets eighty-four clicks from Google.

Who do you think did the best?

Well, Lawyer #1 gets a client within twenty-four hours, and then proceeds to get another twenty-three leads from those fifty clicks.

Lawyer #2 simply gets two inbound calls and zero clients from his eighty-four clicks.

This is a true story of two competing personal injury attorneys.

Lawyer #1 used a "problem first" approach to his advertising, and Lawyer #2, simply sent the traffic to his "good-looking" website.

He just spent a lot of money getting his new website up and running and didn't see the need for a landing page. His website, of course, wasn't designed with the problem first principle in mind.

Have a look at the results of their campaigns:

Lawyer #1: Twenty-three total leads from fifty visitors. That's a conversion rate of 46%.

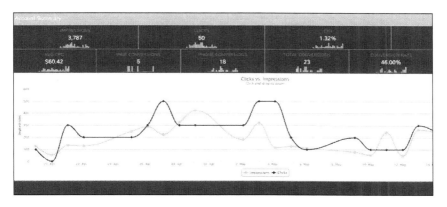

So, 46% of all of the people who saw this attorney's page became a lead.

Lawyer #2: Two leads from eighty-four visitors. That's a conversion rate of 2.38%.

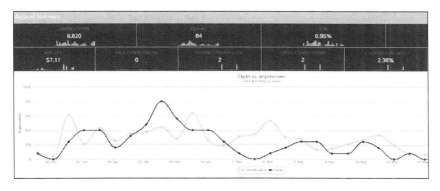

Letting prospects know you understand their problem out-performs a more self-serving approach.

The same is true with every single area of law. To date I have personally witnessed this kind of result for:

- Personal Injury
- DUI
- Estate Planning
- Evictions & Housing
- Criminal Law
- Family Law
- Tax Attorneys
- Bankruptcy
- Divorce
- Business Law
- Immigration

I often speak to attorneys who are convinced that Google advertising doesn't work. They have tried it before, and it gave them zero results. Just like Lawyer #2.

However, there are thousands of attorneys right now making it big with Google ads.

A lot of them are like Lawyer #1. They consistently pull in new clients every single week, all because they focus on the specific problem their visitors are facing.

Don't forget, the problem first approach isn't simply there to help you with advertising. It can be used in every single facet of your law firm. Every single time prospects come across your firm, it will confirm that you understand their problems better than anyone else.

Unfortunately, most attorneys in America do not think about the prospect or their client when advertising themselves.

For example. I did a simple search for a divorce attorney on Justia, in the Phoenix, Arizona, area. This is what I found:

Both of these premium listings have one thing in common, and both are horribly wrong. As you can see, I have blacked out their identities to protect their privacy.

The first listing says:

> *[Attorney Name] has over 35 years of legal experience and has helped thousands of Arizonans with their family law matters, including divorce, child custody, child support, child relocation and alimony.*

The second listing says:

> *[Law office name] is a small boutique firm focused on Divorce, Family Law and Child Custody with six offices in the Greater Phoenix area. Whether you're facing a divorce, custody battle, or spousal support.*

Do any of these listings talk about the prospects and their problem? No.

Do they stand out from each other in any way? No.

They effectively say the same thing. They talk about themselves. A potential client will end up picking the attorney with the best picture or smile. It'll have nothing to do with their experience.

In the U.S. there are hundreds of thousands of attorneys with decades of experience, there are tens of thousands of attorneys with more than one law office, and there are hundreds of thousands who have helped "thousands of clients."

None of those talking points are service winners. None of them are out of the ordinary.

This kind of mediocre language attorneys are using leads to mediocre results. It is a gift to the super attorney who knows how to talk to potential clients.

Look at the results of a study conducted by Wordstream.

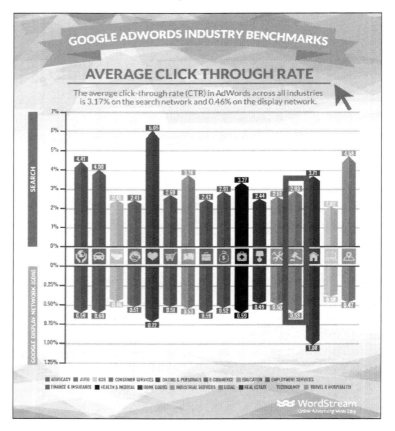

I put a red square over the legal industry's numbers. This shows that the average ad in the industry gets a conversion rate of just 2.93%.

In other words, out of one hundred people who see the webpage of the attorney, less than three people would become a lead.

Compare that to this criminal attorney, who is using the problem first advertising approach:

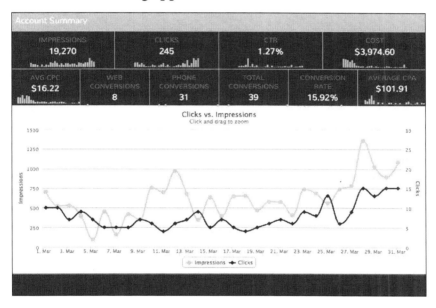

The conversion rate on this webpage is 15.92%. **That is a 443% improvement on the industry average**.

In this example, by using the problem first approach, an attorney is able to capture over 400% more clients with the same advertising budget.

In other words, a *super attorney* spent $3,974.60 to get thirty-one inbound calls, whereas the *average attorney* would need to spend $21,582.07 get the same number of leads.

Like I said before, this happens in all areas of law. When you focus on the problem of the client, instead of focusing on yourself, the improvement in the results is remarkable.

Here is another example, this time for a divorce attorney:

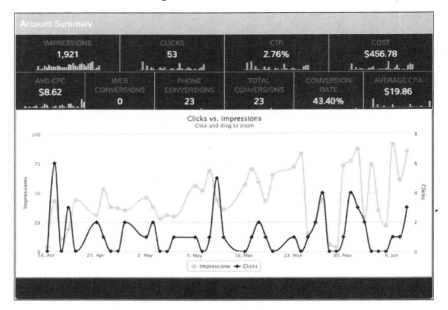

The conversion rate on this campaign is a whopping 43.40%. That is 1,381% higher than the industry average.

The average attorney would have to spend more than ten times as much on advertising to get the same result.

I deliberately used a small campaign budget on this one to give you a taste of what is possible. This was a simple test to show an attorney who didn't believe me when I told him about the results he could get.

I have dozens and dozens of examples I can show you, including one for an immigration attorney who is getting a conversion rate of 28.77%, just under ten times better than the industry average.

Have a look at the following image to see the results.

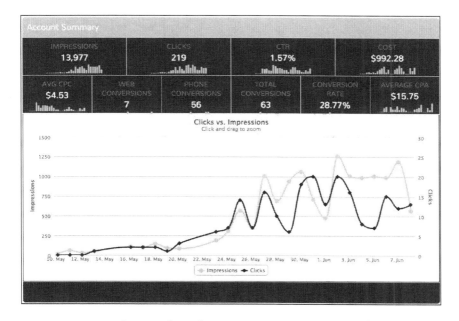

It is no coincidence that these campaigns are working better than industry averages. Don't forget, they are based on rigorous testing. We've tested over 5,000 different marketing messages, with 100,000 ads, and over 1.5 million leads.

The science is as clear as day. **Problem first advertising works.**

On the following page is another example for a family law office. They are getting a 19.03% conversion rate. A six-fold increase over the industry standard.

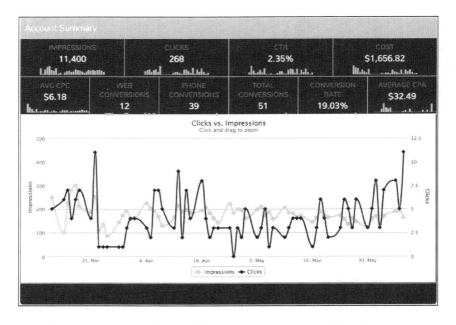

The list goes on and on. The conversion rate for this Personal Injury attorney is **nine times better than the industry average**.

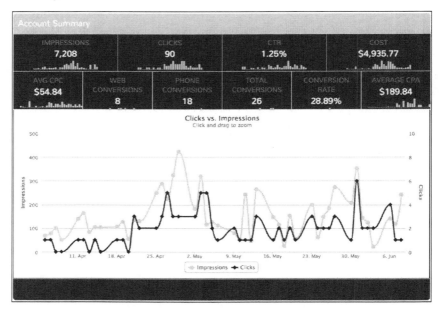

In the next chapter, I'll show you real world examples of what the problem first approach looks like. You'll see practical examples of what is being used right now by the super attorneys out there.

So far, the statistics I have shown you above are small campaigns. They are attorneys who spend $3,000–10,000 per month on advertising. Many attorneys are living a fantastic life, consistently growing their law firms while acquiring new clients every week.

They never have to worry about where the next client is going to come from. They know the phone will keep ringing with new appointments.

Later on in the book, I'll show you how some campaigns do $100,000–300,000 per month in advertising spending. They are making fat profits.

Whether you are a small office that is looking to expand slowly but profitably, or someone who has ambitions to be a multi-office, multi-state law firm, there will be something for you.

Hopefully by now you understand how important it is to think about your prospects first.

Think about their needs above your own experience. Talking about yourself will turn you into a commodity. You'll be like every other attorney out there. The coming waves of change in the industry will swallow you whole. You will be left behind like the 200,000 handlooms in the 1800s.

Now, let's dive into the details of how to execute a problem first advertising campaign.

CHAPTER 9

Your "Unfair Advantage" That'll Turn Visitors into Clients

"Take up one idea. Make that one idea your life—think of it, dream of it, live on that idea. Let the brain, muscles, nerves, every part of your body be full of that idea, and just leave every other idea alone. This is the way to success."

Swami Vivekananda (1863–1902), Famous Indian Hindu monk, a chief disciple of the nineteenth-century Indian mystic Ramakrishna

WHAT I'M ABOUT to reveal is perhaps the best kept "non-secret" of the internet. Attorneys ignore it at their peril. Marketers ignore it because they are lazy.

I found out about it from a guy named Jeff. I haven't met him personally, but like many others, I used his techniques to get extraordinary results. It turns out it works better in the attorney market than any other. More on that in a minute.

In 1994 Jeff was an ordinary thirty-year-old working himself to an early grave on Wall Street. One Wednesday morning he got a research paper from one of the analysts at his firm. Inside of the paper, it stated that internet usage was growing at 2,300% per year.

Jeff quit his job and started working from his garage. Within two months he was making $20,000 per week in sales.

He was obsessed with testing. He tested button colors, page layouts, text, images, how the users scrolled their mouse over his website, eye tracking tests, etc.

Instead of taking a profit, Jeff decided to raise $8 million from Kleiner Perkins (a Venture Capitalist firm) in 1995.

By 1999 he was named *Time* magazine's "Person of the Year." More recently, he was in the news for having a net worth of more than $100 billion. His little obsession with testing created Amazon.

On July 28, 2017, he said:

"If you double the number of experiments you do per year you're going to double your inventiveness."

In other words, the more you test and tweak, the better your results will be.

I've run over 5,000 marketing tests and experiments. Some of those tests would have 20,000 visitors thrown at them per day.

On top of that, we've also bought data from other people's tests. I have an archive of over 1 million different advertising variations and experiments.

This is effectively the "get out of jail free" card of the internet. It is a shortcut to success. It is your new unfair advantage.

You don't have time to figure out what works and what doesn't. You are an attorney, not a data geek who spends eight hours a day looking at statistics.

When you have an ad running on Google and people click on it, the page they land on is referred to as a "landing page."

Remember in the previous chapter I showed you how the landing pages we use get anywhere between 300–1,300% more leads and clients than the industry average?

A big part of the reason is the "problem first" approach. Now within that approach there are thousands of different head-lines, layouts, images, and colors you can use.

After a few thousand tests, we have found the following lay-out to perform incredibly well.

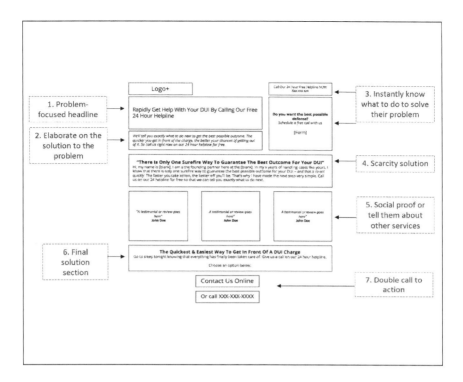

1. Problem-focused headline:

We found that you get the best results when the headline confirms that the prospects are in the right place. For whatever reason, as humans we're constantly doubting whether or not we are in the right place.

You need to address that. In this example, you can see that we talk about helping them with a DUI specifically. We do not say "criminal law" or anything about the attorney. We're jumping straight to the point on this one.

Remember, your prospects have a problem, and confirming that you can help them with that problem is your top priority. Shortly, I'll go into more depth about what makes a great headline.

2. Elaborate on the solution to the problem:

This goes directly below the headline. It talks about the solution to their big problem and the very next steps they should take. In every instance, the solution to their problem is YOU, the attorney.

3. Instantly know what to do to solve their problem:

The phone number is right at the top and quickly visible. To solve their problem, they either pick up the phone to call you, or complete the online form. So, by quickly skimming the page, they'll know exactly what action to take next.

In a minute I'll show you what this looks like on a real page.

4. Scarcity:

This helps people to take action faster. It lets the visitors know that there is only one surefire way to get the best possible outcome. *And that is to act quickly and be prepared.* The quicker they act, the more likely they are to come out on top.

People love to procrastinate. It is your job to ensure that they understand the consequences of doing so. The scarcity section outlines that.

5. Social proof or "other services":

This section adds credibility in the form of testimonials and case studies. It reassures the visitors that you can indeed solve their problem. If you don't have any testimonials, then you can list the other services you provide here.

Remember our chapter on reviews? They can make or break your law firm. Having some to place in this section demonstrates only one of the ways in which you can use them.

6. Final solution section:

This section tells the visitors that the quickest and easiest way to solve their specific problem is to get in touch with you. It is the final call to action and plays on their desire to get things under control again.

One of the worst fears people have is for something to spiral out of control. We hear horror stories about legal problems that have piled up for people.

7. Double call to action:

This gives the visitors two choices. Either they can call, or they should fill out the online form. Both of them go straight to your office so that you can take on the new case.

Can you see how much attention to detail has been put into this layout? You can't simply "guess" what's going to work and what you need to say.

You have to follow a specific formula that urges the visitors to take action. Experimenting and testing is the only way to truly find out what works.

On the following page is an example of what a page could look like for you:

About a year before writing the very words on this page, one of our tests threw up a new variation that gives us even better results.

By adding a brief article with useful information underneath the reviews, we found ourselves gaining even more trust with visitors. This pushed up the conversion rate and even lowered the advertising costs. Google rewarded us with cheaper clicks.

This page has all seven elements the previous page has but with content added below the three boxes.

People who are still unsure need more information, so we give it to them. This is a fantastic place to get rid of some of their fears.

Right next to the content you can see even more reviews. This reinforces their belief that you are the authority. You, and you alone, can help them solve this big problem they have.

Now, when it comes to attracting visitors who are reading the content on your page, you need to be crystal clear on their next step.

Most attorneys understand that the legal process isn't always easy, quick or clear-cut.

And that's fine, but you don't have to throw it in your visitors' faces. Your visitors aren't on this page because they are about to face all the legal challenges in the world.

They are on this page because they want to know what their legal options are. They need an attorney to help them figure stuff out.

And getting that help is easy, simple, quick, and painless. All they have to do is pick up the phone and the process has begun.

Here are some more examples:

RAPIDLY TAKE COMPLETE CONTROL OF YOUR DIVORCE CASE

Get your FREE one-on-one consultation now so that you can get the best possible outcome for your divorce.

This tells the clients that you are going to help them get control back in their lives, and you are going to do it quickly.

Most attorneys believe that the clients are only satisfied once the case is done.

That is not true. Simply by outlining a plan for them, or a few options, they already feel at ease. Therefore, helping them to "rapidly take control" isn't as far-fetched as it seems.

Here's another example:

RAPIDLY GET HELP WITH YOUR DUI TODAY

We'll tell you exactly what to do next to get the best possible outcome. The quicker you get in front of the charge, the better your chances of getting out of it. So call us right now for a free consultation.

By simply picking up the phone and taking advantage of your free consultation, the prospects have already got some help with their DUI. That is as rapid as it gets.

Pointing out these "obvious" perks in your advertising makes all the difference. The testing has shown it to be the case. The more obvious something seems to you, the more likely it is you should point it out on your website.

People love being reassured that something will be quick, easy, painless, and worth their time. Picking up the phone to call an attorney ticks all of those boxes. The actual legal case might not be quick and easy, but calling you is. So, make sure they know it.

Most prospects procrastinate because they fear the overall process. They are out of the depth and they are worried about it. That's why it is essential to make them understand how easy and quick it is to simply dial a number or fill out a form.

Here's one last example of a headline to drive home the point:

IF YOU OR A LOVED ONE HAS SUFFERED DOMESTIC ABUSE, GIVE US A CALL TODAY FOR A FREE CONSULTATION

Rapidly get help with your case from some of the best attorneys in California.

Everything is quick, free, and easy.

Got it?

Good.

Let's take a quick look at how you will use what we've learned so far to get new clients calling you up every week.

1. You will focus on their problems, not your own achievements.

2. You will use a landing page with a layout that has been tested.

3. You will get them to understand that the next step is quick, simple, and solves their immediate problem.

Since you're an attorney, you may have guessed that there is more to it. And you are right, there is.

Most law offices' advertising efforts are woefully inadequate. Don't worry, the next steps are not difficult or complicated. They are simply some of the industry's best kept secrets.

You'll discover how you can lower your average advertising cost by 30–50%. You'll learn how to bring back lost clients who have said, "No," without needing text messages or emails. And so much more.

CHAPTER 10

How to Create Hyper-Specific Advertising that Quickly Gives You Piping Hot Leads

"What we need to do is always lean into the future; when the world changes around you and when it changes against you—what used to be a tail wind is now a head wind—you have to lean into that and figure out what to do because complaining isn't a strategy."

Jeff Bezos (1964), Founder of Amazon. com and worth over $100 billion

"Advertising doesn't work."

"You're right," I replied.

"So there's no point in me doing it," the attorney continues.

"You're absolutely right," I replied.

The attorney stares at me for a moment with a confused look on his face and says, *"But isn't that what you do for attorneys?"*

"Yes, it is a big part of what I do."

I was sitting at a restaurant in Scottsdale, Arizona, with a criminal lawyer. He made his views to me abundantly clear. He's tried several different marketing firms, and he's got nothing from it. According to him, it is all a waste of time.

He was taken aback by my answers. I agreed with everything he said, because he spoke the truth.

At first, he thought I was about to confess to something he was suspecting all along. He thought that marketing firms promise the world and don't deliver. He believed that they are there to make a quick buck and send you packing when things don't work out.

He started telling me a story of how he hired one of the biggest Google advertising firms in the country. They had over 50,000 clients, their price was reasonable, and to top it off they won prizes from the Chamber of Commerce for being one of the fastest growing medium sized companies in America.

Yet, once he paid them, he felt like they wasted his money. He spent $1,000 per month and got nothing from it.

What's the point? His solution was to keep relying on referrals and organic Google searches for his leads.

So he sat there. Waiting for me to make a confession. Waiting for me to reveal the scam. Waiting in anticipation to be vindicated.

After all, I have just agreed with everything he said. What could my answer possibly be, other than it is all a "big scam"?

Instead of going head-to-head with him, and explaining to him about problem first advertising, how law firms were different from other businesses, and if you pay peanuts you get monkeys, I decided to pull out a little booklet. In this booklet, I had dozens and dozens of comments from attorneys. For example, here's one from a guy named Jason B:

Gary is probably the most important connection I have made in the last 10 years. He has become the guru on the mountaintop for all of our legal marketing needs. His understanding of attraction marketing using the crocodile brain and mass marketing system have proven to deliver amazing results. He has been able to help us create better sales processes, attract better clients and grow our legal financing platform by leaps and bounds. Gary is like a college professor that can take complex subjects and simplify them in a way anyone could understand. 10/10 would recommend if you are looking for more clients, who are ready to hire you before they ever meet you.

Here is another one from an attorney named Zaid:

Very knowledgeable on marketing. They actually take a different approach to marketing rather than the same old approach by other companies. They actually focus on the psychology of the consumer rather than throwing template adds out on the web that make you look the same as everyone else.

And the list went on and on. All of them attorneys who were killing it advertising on the very same platform he believed would never work.

He then came across this review from a PI attorney named Don:

As a PI attorney you know I get marketed to all the time and unfortunately over the years I never found that elite marketing expert that really knows exactly how to market and grow my law practice. Fortunately, that all changed the day I met Gary and started working with Big Mouth Marketing. From the beginning Gary was very patient and it was clear that he was laser focused on my best interest, a refreshing change from others that just wanted to sell me something! He took the time to learn about my practice in great detail. It was abundantly clear from day one that his goal was to help grow my practice. Any attorney that is ready to grow their practice owes it to themselves to have a conversation with a true marketing expert and a gracious genuine man.

When he read these reviews from other attorneys, he became even more confused.

Why would I agree that advertising didn't work and then show him all of these comments? Was I simply playing him in some way?

The answer is no. I wasn't playing him. I do agree that advertising doesn't work for the vast majority of attorneys. In fact, I would go as far to say that advertising doesn't work for all attorneys in the country.

Why?

Well, straight up advertising on Google or any other platform is a waste of time and money. Without testing market specific messaging, ads, and landing pages, it is useless.

And even then, you need other systems in place, like Passive Return Agents, to bring the average cost down and cement your authority in the prospect's mind (more on them in a minute).

But by far, one of the biggest reasons advertising doesn't work for attorneys is because their ads are vague and do not talk about the prospect's problem.

We've covered this in the previous chapter when it comes to landing pages and webpages.

Let me show you how attorneys are wasting their advertising budgets.

A quick note before I get started. If you find yourself reading this book and your firm's name appears as a bad example of advertising, know that I am not trying to insult you or belittle your efforts.

There is no way for you to know exactly what works and what doesn't. In my lifetime, I have spent multiple millions buying ads. It is my obsession to find out how to best grow law firms. It is my full-time job. Just like it is yours to study and practice being an attorney for all those years, it is my job to figure out how to grow your law practice.

Ok, so with that out of the way, at the risk of offending someone, here is an example of a bad ad:

Holth & Kollman, LLC | Trial Lawyers | holthkollman.com ᵈ
[Ad] www.holthkollman.com/ ▾ +1 860-447-0331
Free Consultation. Trusted by New London County residents for over 40 yrs. Highlights: 45+ Years Of Experience, Free Consultation Available.
Estate Planning Law · Personal Injury Law · Family Law · Bankruptcy Law · Real Estate Law
♀ 06320, 58 Huntington St, New London, CT

By looking at this ad, can you guess what the Google search was?

Most probably not. Let's try and figure it out together.

The headline, the URL, and the description give nothing away. It doesn't talk about the problem the prospect is facing. There is no way for us to know what on earth the firm is advertising.

Imagine coming across an ad that advertises water:

We have water. Lots of water. Enjoy water.

We've been handling water for 25+ years. We are trusted by people who also love water. Come and experience water.

Do you know what they are promoting?

Is it a water park? A store that sells water? Or a water utility company? Or perhaps it is a PADI diving center?

Just like the water industry, the legal industry is vast, and people are confused. You need to speak directly to them.

So, from this ad, let's try and figure out what I typed into Google to get this served to me.

The only clue we have is at the bottom in a section we call "Google extensions."

Holth & Kollman, LLC | Trial Lawyers | holthkollman.com ⚖

[Ad] www.holthkollman.com/ ▾ +1 860-447-0331

Free Consultation. Trusted by New London County residents for over 40 yrs. Highlights: 45+ Years Of Experience, Free Consultation Available.

| Estate Planning Law · Personal Injury Law · Family Law · Bankruptcy Law · Real Estate Law |

📍 06320, 58 Huntington St, New London, CT

From this, you may assume I searched either for an *estate planning, PI, family, bankruptcy*, or *real estate* attorney.

If you assumed it was one of these areas of law, you would be *wrong*.

Here is a screenshot from the search:

As someone who is looking for a DUI attorney, who do you think I would choose?

The first ad isn't perfect, but at least it mentions the word "DUI." If you had a bad back and needed surgery. Would you hire the back surgeon or the doctor that says he helps with headaches, coughs, and general illnesses?

You can actually buy the advertising data these firms are using. And I can see that the top law firm, that is specific to DUI, spends three times more on adverting than the bottom firm with the vague ad.

It isn't because they have more money to burn or that they simply feel generous to Google. It is because they are getting more leads and clients. Therefore, they can spend more on marketing.

The top three DUI advertisers in the U.S. are:

- DrunkDrivingLawyers.com – $90,000 per month
- DUI.com – $58,600 per month
- DUIAttorneyGroup.com – $65,000 per month

Let's take a look at some of their ads.

Do you notice how specific that ad is?

It asks a question that the prospect immediately says, "Yes!" to.

Arrested for a DUI in CA? – DUI.com

Remember to be as specific as possible for the keywords being typed into the search bar.

Here are some more ads they are running:

Las Vegas DUI Attorney

Want your DUI Dismissed?? Call Now.

Save your License. Free Visit.

Best DUI Lawyer Philadelphia

Don't Let a DUI Ruin Your Life

Call Now to Save Your License.

St Petersburg DUI Arrest?

You Only Have 10 Days to Fight a DUI Offense!

Call Us to Avoid Jail

Are you starting to notice the "problem first" approach here? Every single ad talks about the specific problem they are facing in the city or town they are facing them.

When you hire a firm that deals with 50,000 businesses from all walks of life they won't be doing this. They simply don't have the man power for this kind of in-depth analysis and testing.

They charge too little. It is the equivalent of going to Rocket Lawyer for a $50 contract template versus getting an actual experienced attorney to help you one-on-one for thousands of dollars.

LEGALLY STEALING STRATEGIES FROM THE MOST PROFITABLE ADVERTISERS & AVOIDING MISTAKES

This reminds me of a video I saw a few years back. A female cheetah was stalking her prey in Tanzania. She had two cubs with her and called them over so that they could observe how she hunted.

She was careful and calculated. The two cubs were rather large and helped the mother to take down an impala.

They tried to choke out the impala, but it was too big and strong.

After a few seconds, the impala broke loose and swung its horns. One of the cheetahs got critically injured and couldn't chase after it. The other two chased but quickly realized it was useless.

Months later, the surviving cheetahs were about to make the same mistake as their mother.

Just before they started chasing another adult impala, the other one growled and stopped the chase in its tracks.

They learned from their previous mistake and, instead, picked out a newborn baby. It was easier prey, and they didn't need to risk their lives.

You don't only have to learn from **your** mistakes, you can just as easily learn from **someone else's**, like these cheetahs.

Although cheetahs are the fastest animal in the wild, have incredible eyesight, and have ferocious instinct, they can still learn from the mistakes of others.

Just because I have overseen millions in ad spending, generated well over 1.5 million leads, run over 100,000 advertisements, and conducted 5,000 marketing tests, doesn't mean I can't keep learning from the mistakes of others.

That's why I constantly buy data, and lots of it.

I can peek under the hood of some of the biggest advertisers in the industry.

Picture this.

Pretend you are a huge PI firm. You have been spending $300,000 per month on advertising for seven years.

You've got a big, fat budget, and you can afford to make mistakes.

So you test out different platforms and keywords, and you continually tweak your ads to get the best possible results.

You've run over 500,000 variations, using computer simulations and experiments.

You'd feel on top of the world as all the hot PI leads come knocking on your door every day.

You know exactly what works and what doesn't. No guesswork.

What if I told you it is possible for you have that data?

For example, here are three of the biggest PI Google advertisers in the country:

- AccidentAttorneys.com – $97,000 per month
- Lawyers.com – $123,000 per month
- InjuryHelpLine.com – $257,000 per month

They are currently bidding on 131,946 different search terms in Google.

However, if you overlap all of their phrases and see which ones they have in common, you'll see this:

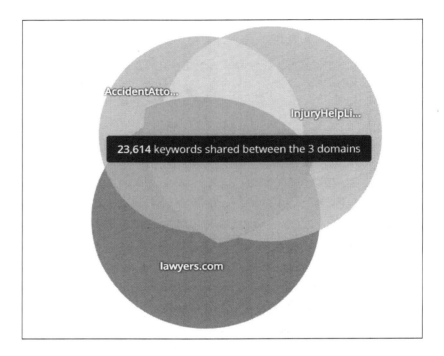

In all of their tests, we know that Americans type in 23,614 core searches when it comes to PI cases.

These search terms are so profitable that all the biggest advertisers are bidding on them.

Also, AccidentAttorneys.com has tested a total of 60,888 different ads. We can take a peak where they've spent the most money. This'll tell us how successful these ads are.

For example, they spend a huge amount on the keyword "*Auto accident lawyer.*"

In the last few months they have tested hundreds of variations. The most successful were these three:

AD #1:

AD #2:

AD #3:

It turns out that adding "(Recommended)" in the ad increased the click-through rate and lowered the advertising costs. I just saved myself months, or possibly years, of work by making use of the biggest advertiser's data.

Let's take a look at another experiment that the biggest DUI advertisers in the country did and what they settled on.

Here's a recent experiment DrunkDrivingLawyers.com ran.

The biggest keyword they target is **"DUI Defense."**

AD #1

AD #2:

AD #3:

Ad #2 was the winner.

We have access to all 18,382 of their ads. So, we can compare and see which ones work and which ones don't.

Then we compile that with our data and get results that are unheard of in the industry.

By the way, this is one advertiser out of thousands we have data on. Companies that use data will get much better results than those that ignore it.

Remember in the beginning of this book?

I told you that things will change so rapidly that only the super attorneys will survive. Using data like this, and having access to thousands of experiments, is another small glimpse into that future.

Super attorneys will hire companies that make sure of all the technologies available to them. Lagging attorneys will continue to rely on word of mouth until their times run out.

A recent study commissioned by Microsoft has quantified the difference between data leaders and the so-called "laggards," who are less mature in their use of data.

The average S&P 500 company that uses data effectively makes $100 million more per year.

The same is true of smaller businesses, like law firms. Their average gross profit margin on goods and services is 18% greater than the laggards'.

So, back to the attorney I was talking to at the beginning of this chapter. He told me that advertising doesn't work, and I agreed with him. For the vast majority of attorneys, advertising doesn't work.

For advertising to work, you need to be a pro (or hire a pro). You need to test thousands of variations every single month. You need to analyze the thousands of variations all the competition tests every month. You need data scientists to make sure everything is statistically valid.

And then finally, you need to record every single outcome to know how many cases came from each experiment.

As you can see, the top advertisers in the industry are using these very same methods to churn out huge results.

They are the top 1% out there. However, you can do even better. You can surpass even them. In the next chapter, I'll show you how. Hold on to your horses; things are about to get real.

CHAPTER 11

The Authority Advertising Model

"You can't connect the dots looking forward; you can only connect them looking backwards. So you have to trust that the dots will somehow connect in your future. You have to trust in something—your gut, destiny, life, karma, whatever. This approach has never let me down, and it has made all the difference in my life."

Steve Jobs (1955–2011), Founder of Apple Inc

A FEW YEARS ago, I was walking around the mall and saw a Footlocker store. It was right outside the restrooms, where I was waiting for my friend.

"Do you want to buy these shoes?" asked the salesman.

"Not now, thank you," I replied.

An hour later, I walked past the same store, and the sales guy said the same thing.

"Do you want to buy these shoes?"

I thought to myself, "*How weird for this guy to ask me the exact same question, with the exact same lame sales pitch.*"

He probably didn't realize that he'd asked me before. He must see hundreds of people pass by every hour.

And then a thought struck me. That single thought ended up being responsible for millions in additional clients for attorneys across the country.

You see, when people search for an attorney, they genuinely NEED one. It isn't something people just "do" in their spare time.

Once someone clicks on your ad and visits your website, there is a very good chance he has the potential to become a client.

However, as you can see from the previous chapters, only 2–3% of people take the next action.

That means 97–98% of people who see your sales pitch say "no."

Obviously, using the landing page templates I revealed to you in this book get better results than that (you've seen the proof), yet the point remains.

People say "no" way more often than they say "yes."

In the past, this was ok. We only need a small percentage of people to say "yes" for you to make good money.

However, as advertising costs started creeping up, people came up with ingenious ways to improve their results.

For example, one of the most successful tactics was retargeting.

In its most basic form, when you click on an ad online and visit a website, you'll get followed around (annoyingly) on every single other website you go to.

For example:

You visit Footlocker.com, and then you read an article on CNN. All of a sudden, you see an ad for Footlocker. And you see that same ad over and over again on different websites.

It follows you around like a stalker, constantly asking you to buy their shoes.

It is kind of like that Footlocker salesman but on overdrive. Imagine you go into Footlocker, and you say *"no"* to the salesman.

Then you go into McDonalds, and there that same guy is again, asking you to buy shoes *again*.

Then you go to another town entirely and stop at the library. And sure enough, this same salesman is there trying to sell you shoes with the same sales pitch.

Even while you are having a BBQ with your friends, this guy keeps rearing his annoying head.

No matter what you do or where you go, this salesman is following you around with the same sales pitch.

Attorneys are using this method all the time. Although it worked wonders in 2011, it is draining their bank accounts today.

When that Footlocker salesman asked me the second time, a thought occurred to me. Asking me over and over again if I want the same thing after saying *"no"* made me more determined to say *"no"* again.

So if 97% of people say *"no"* to your sales pitch in the form of your website, why are marketing companies constantly hitting those prospects with the same sales pitch over and over again.

If you look at this, it is a direct sales pitch for your services:

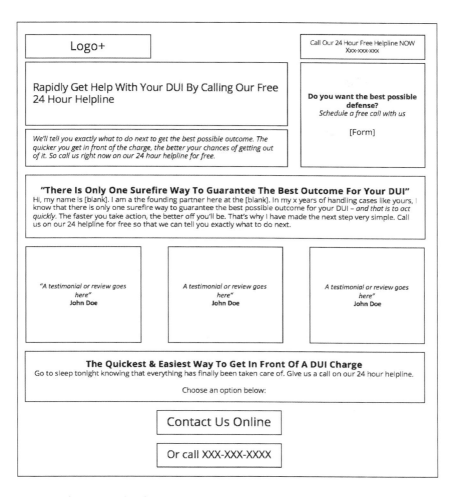

What if, instead of a sales pitch, you send them something of value?

The best way to illustrate how this works is to put yourself in the shoes of your prospect (pun intended).

Once somebody visits Google and searches "DUI attorney [city]" and clicks on your ad, you **know** that he wants and need a lawyer.

Why else would he stop binge watching Netflix to search for something that he has no real desire for?

Bingo! He has a problem that needs solving. And Google was his answer.

Just because the user doesn't respond to the "sales pitch" in your ad doesn't mean he doesn't need a lawyer.

It means he is procrastinating.

In the past you would have paid for that click and lost him forever. By the time he feels like contacting you again, he has forgotten who you are.

So, here's what you do to make sure that never happens.

Now that you know that person is interested in finding a DUI attorney, and you know he is on the fence, you can send him something a little different.

When he visits your landing page, you can "tag" his browser.

This allows you to place ads in front of him throughout the next few weeks.

Instead of annoying him with ads, we're going to smack him in the face with information that helps to alleviate the problem he is facing.

We're going to do this by posting an article in his Facebook newsfeed.

Here's a quick example.

I go to Google and type in *"DUI attorney Phoenix."*

I get cold feet for some reason and decide to watch cat videos on Facebook.

Next thing I see is a helpful article specifically speaking to the problem I have in my Facebook newsfeed.

It is an article in my Facebook newsfeed.

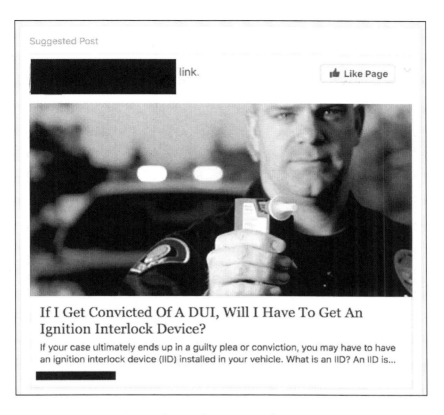

link.

👍 Like Page

If I Get Convicted Of A DUI, Will I Have To Get An Ignition Interlock Device?

If your case ultimately ends up in a guilty plea or conviction, you may have to have an ignition interlock device (IID) installed in your vehicle. What is an IID? An IID is...

Imagine you are searching for a DUI lawyer and then this article pops up on your favorite website.

Would you consider it useful?

How about this?

We call this a *Passive Return Agent (PRA)*. Instead of bludgeoning your prospects to death with the same sales pitch over and over, you decide to help them with a simple 500-word article.

This stays true to the problem first approach to advertising. It also comes with the added benefit of solidifying your authority in the particular area of law they are interested in.

Not only did they see your ads in Google, but now they are seeing you all over Facebook with helpful articles. When they finally decide to pick up the phone and call an attorney, who do you think they'll think of first?

And it doesn't stop there.

Below you can see an illustration of what is happening.

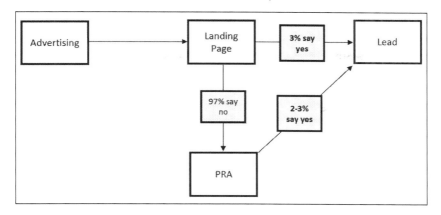

Now we've potentially doubled the number of prospects reaching out to you. And what most people don't know is that you can carry this process on for up to six months.

Remember, people procrastinate. In some cases, it takes months for them to finally pick up the phone and call you.

So, we add another Passive Return Agent and push it out to them the month after on Facebook.

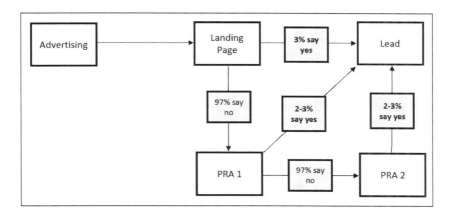

After six months, the entire advertising funnel looks like this:

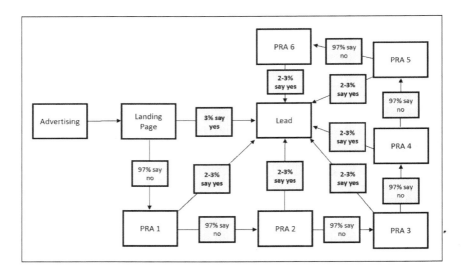

This is called the Crocodile Close. As you can see, once you've identified a prospect who needs an attorney, you're going to take hold of him and help him for as long as he lets you.

Just like a crocodile who patiently waits for its prey, this does not let go of the prospect. However, instead of killing and eating your prospect, you'll be helping him, and in turn feed This is called the Crocodile Close. As you can see, once you've identified a prospect who needs an attorney, you're going to take hold of him and help him for as long as he lets you.

Just like a crocodile who patiently waits for its prey, this does not let go of the prospect. However, instead of killing and eating your prospect, you'll be helping him, and in turn feed the growth of your law firm.

Are you starting to see why advertising does NOT work for the average attorney?

Do you believe that every single advertiser out there puts this much thought into their campaigns?

Sadly, you'll probably agree that they do not.

Like I said at the beginning of this book, times are changing. Everything is getting more sophisticated, and technology will leave tens of thousands of attorneys out of business.

They will not be able to keep up with this rapidly changing environment. However, you shouldn't worry. A period of rapid change always gives rise to rapid opportunity.

Right now, while reading this book, you have an opportunity to lead yourself to greatness. With the information you have at your disposal right now, you could take complete control over how much and how fast your law firm grows.

You can be the one who snaps up struggling attorneys and start covering vast areas of law without doing much of the extra work.

By embracing this information, you now have a choice.

Choice #1:

You can choose to live comfortably by deploying these techniques. You can stay slightly ahead of the pack and enjoy a life as a highly profitable attorney. It is a pretty good life and one that many attorneys that have these tools at their disposal pick.

Or...

You have choice #2:

You can grow your law firm. You can become one of the super attorneys with vast resources, wealth, and staff at your disposal. You can even go from being a small, regional player to dominating your state.

I'll even give you a checklist later for growing your law firm across state lines. Turning yourself into a national giant isn't impossible.

Essentially, you now have some of the tools necessary to decide your fate. You can choose how big and how successful you want to be. You no longer need to feel like there are elements out of your control.

Instead of your competition, the market, or technology dictating what you can do and how high you can reach, you now have that power.

Remaining a profitable small firm is totally fine. It is your choice.

Becoming a medium sized profitable firm is fine too. It is your choice.

Turning yourself into a super firm that stretches across state lines is also your choice.

The point is you have the freedom to grow as much and as fast as you want.

Nobody can take that choice away from you.

However, that is only the case if you take action. If you ignore all of the growth strategies mentioned in this book, then you will watch as your competition has the choice to grow.

In the next chapter we're going to cover another growth strategy. This will help you to dominate your local Google and Bing listing.

And as always, most attorneys are ignoring this low hanging fruit at their own risk.

CHAPTER 12

How to Grow Your Law Firm while Working Less

"To enjoy life, you don't need fancy nonsense, but you do need to control your time and realize that most things just aren't as serious as you make them out to be."

Tim Ferris (1977), American author of *The 4-Hour Work Week*, entrepreneur, and public speaker

IF YOU WERE to describe Gregory M. Owens to aspiring law school graduates, they would start getting excited.

Mr. Owens was a partner at a global law firm, White & Case. He graduated from university and immediately started earning a fat paycheck.

Yet, on New Year's Eve 2013, at the age of fifty-five, he filed for bankruptcy.

According to his petition, he had $400 in his checking account and $400 in savings. His clothes were worth an estimated $900, and his watch was worthless because it was broken.

How could a man getting anywhere between $350,000–500,000 per year be in a situation like this?

The answer may not surprise you; however, the lesson it holds for other attorneys, like you, *will*.

What happened to Mr. Owens has a direct correlation with a secret that will make you incredibly rich one day, while working less.

Perhaps the path you are going down right now is a good fit for you.

Or perhaps you are like the vast majority of attorneys out there who realize they need some kind of change.

"The unhappiest job in America is an associate attorney."

Those are the words I read in a Forbes post a few years back. After extensive job satisfaction surveys, attorneys came at the bottom of the list.

I was slightly perplexed. I understand the job can be stressful, but I had no idea there was a lower job satisfaction than that of a cold-calling salesperson.

And to top off my confusion, why would two-thirds of parents want their kids to become attorneys if it apparently means a lifetime of unhappiness?

People who clean toilets are supposedly walking around with bigger smiles than lawyers.

Just ask Mr. Owens.

Yet law schools are overfilled. There are too many kids wanting to become attorneys, and it is going to crush the market in the coming years.

However, it gets even more confusing.

All of these parents who say they want their kids to be attorneys actually really dislike attorneys.

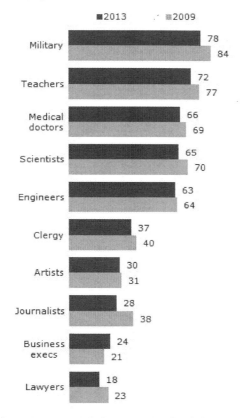

Trend in Perceived Contribution

% saying each group contributes "a lot" to society's well-being

■2013   ■2009

Group	2013	2009
Military	78	84
Teachers	72	77
Medical doctors	66	69
Scientists	65	70
Engineers	63	64
Clergy	37	40
Artists	30	31
Journalists	28	38
Business execs	24	21
Lawyers	18	23

Source: Pew Research Center surveys March 21-April 8, 2013 and April 28-May 12, 2009. Q6a-j. Responses of those who said some, not very much, nothing at all and those who did not give an answer are not shown.

PEW RESEARCH CENTER

Look at the chart above. I read this research back in 2013 and kept the image to this day.

Even banking executives are preferred to attorneys. People somehow believe that attorneys "do not contribute to society."

And it was all summed up nicely by Alison Monahan, a prominent attorney who has looked into these issues a lot. She said that "attorneys are destined to be either miserable, or broke."

Most attorneys believe their happiness lies in making more money, having more free time, and having a pot of cash for security.

And that may be the reason why you picked up this book and are reading the very words on this page.

After all, there is a very detailed and clear blueprint on what you need to do to become a super attorney.

However, so far, this book has not promised you happiness.

Yes, you'll get more clients who are happier with your services.

Yes, you'll get a glowing reputation with five-star reviews elevating you in everyone's minds.

Yes, you'll get more cash up front.

Yes, Yes, Yes, YES!

I have seen them happen. Time and time again. And that may be enough for you.

However, some of it is still hard work. Of course, you could outsource everything to a firm like mine. We'll take care of it, and you won't have to worry.

But there is still work to do.

You still have to be patient. You still have to see clients. You still need to implement what we've talked about in this book.

If you do it right, you can do it with ease.

Your life as an attorney will become much easier and you'll relieve some of the stress you may be feeling.

Yet for some, that is not enough.

Some attorneys want the growth without working more.

Mr. Owens, who went bankrupt at the age of fifty-five while pulling in half a million per year, can attest to the following statement:

"Working harder doesn't mean you gain wealth."

True wealth is being on the golf course and still making money.

True wealth is when you have assets working hard to secure your future.

And that is what Mr. Owens did.

He was the asset, *but he was someone else's asset.*

What if I told you that you could grow your law firm into a self-running firm? Something that makes cash, year in, year out? An asset that you can sell at any time for a large pot of cash?

Have you thought about what you are going to do for retirement?

Have you thought about, perhaps, retiring early?

All of this is well within the realm of the possible.

Because here are the facts:

1. You know how to use financing to get more clients and more cash.

2. You know how to get a glowing reputation.

3. You know how to use follow up systems.

4. You know how to get your staff to answer the phone to get more clients who are happier.

5. You know how to advertise to fill the pipeline with eager new faces who hand over cash for legal services.

6. You know how to get to the top of Google searches to snatch local leads away from your competition.

Now imagine having all that working for you in a firm that takes on clients and churns out high quality cases, all while you are sipping a glass of wine with whoever you want, in the middle of the day.

The next step is to take all of that growth potential and make it a reality without you needing to work harder.

And it is easier than you think. The blueprint is there. Many attorneys have done it, and now it is your turn.

So how do you do it?

Ally Kennedy, the founder of the Association of Mother Immigration Attorneys, puts it this way: *"Become systems dependent and not people dependent."*

Each system that you add to your law firm becomes an asset that pays you over and over again.

The reason why is simple. A system runs itself. A system can be taught by anyone to anyone.

Although we all like to think we are special in our jobs, most of our work can be broken down into a series of linear steps.

Some of those steps require a bit more expertise, but there is always someone that can do them.

For example, there is a company in Silicon Valley that has a special piece of software. It observes all of the tasks of middle management.

It then fires all of the middle management and outsources their tasks to people in cheaper countries with less skill.

Then the software observes those outsources for two years. It proceeds to fire them and then takes over all of the tasks itself.

Just like that, incredibly complicated tasks have been broken down and can now be done by a system that has been put in place.

Don't worry, you won't have to hire a super intelligent AI machine to fire everyone. Not even close.

This is simply an extreme example of how powerful simple processes are.

Here's an example a little closer to home.

What makes a good legal assistant?

Let's say you hire a new assistant named Doug, and he does the following:

1. Creates a questionnaire to gather the exact info you need when a client comes on board

2. Prepares all the papers so that clients simply have to sign the dotted line when they come in

3. Scans all of your mail and sends it to your email so that you can quickly look at what's important without needing to go through physical papers

4. Keeps a detailed call log with who called, what they needed, and how it was resolved

5. And manages to bring you tea and coffee when you want it

You'd think, *"Wow what a great hire."*

Lucky breaks like that hardly ever happen. Yet if you have a system in place that details each one of those tasks, your staff will automatically be Doug, the perfect employee.

Right now, you may be thinking, *"Yeah Gary, that's greeeaaat, but how does that make me rich and spend more time with my family on vacation?"*

Good question.

Here's how.

Once you have systems in place, hiring staff is easy. It even becomes a doodle to hire another attorney. Because guess what? You even have a system in place for hiring and firing staff.

None of it has to be done by you.

STEP 1: DOMINATE ONE AREA OF LAW AT A TIME

So, you are the Superman at marketing your law firm now. You can easily dominate a single area of law.

You may be tempted to run off and promote every area of law you do. Don't.

Relax, and make sure you have the one area you are focusing on right now down to a tee.

Let's say one of the areas of law you specialize in is criminal law.

Break that down into subsections. For example, DUI.

Get a steady stream of DUI clients through the door and have a streamlined system in place to deal with them.

This will massively increase your profitability. Not only will you get more per client because of the strategies in this book, but you will cut the costs of helping the client with processes.

Now your income has gone up, and your costs have gone down. All because you focused on one area of law and streamlined it.

Then, and only then, should you start on the other areas of law you have capabilities in.

STEP 2A: DOMINATE OTHER LOCATIONS

You now have two choices. Expand on the areas of law or expand your locations. Both have their benefits and drawbacks.

So, I'll cover both.

Once you have an area of law streamlined, you may be well served to dominate another location.

I call this the "Skinny Move" because it costs so little to do and gets you paid before making any big investments.

For example, if you have an office in Scottsdale, Arizona, you may want to have an office in Happy Valley too.

You will simply implement the same principles that have made your law office successful in the new location. After all, everything has been systemized (more on that in a minute).

Hire temporary office space from Regus or something similar.

Hire an attorney to see clients in that newly rented office.

You can still route phone calls to your main office. You don't have to duplicate phone answering to multiple offices. That is a recipe for waste.

Once you have clients coming in, you'll find enough money to set up a fully functioning office. Remember, you have systems for everything, so the move can be done by your office manager.

That's why it is called a *skinny move.*

You can do this all over the state. Before you know it, you can have a dozen or more profitable law offices that work on one area of law, while you simply manage them (if you want to). You can even hire a CEO to do that.

Trust me when I say that other attorneys will look at you with extreme admiration mixed with jealousy.

And it doesn't have to stop there. You can even move beyond your state. You simply need to hire attorneys who are bar qualified wherever you want to move.

STEP 2B: DOMINATE OTHER AREA OF LAW

This step is slightly harder than the previous step. By sticking to one area of law, you can duplicate the processes. Your staff become very specialized and can easily implement in another location.

However, if you want to become one of the richest attorneys in the country, you can start this step after the specialization of a specific area of law is complete.

Naturally, getting four areas of law working for you is roughly four times the profit. However, things get more complicated, and your staffing costs rise. It is easier to mix things up and make a mistake. Therefore, having systems in place becomes more important than ever.

You might even want to have different departments to handle each area so that you can individually streamline each area of law.

1. Hire an attorney who is qualified in that area of law.

2. Set up the marketing and advertising systems you are outsourcing.

3. Get clients and implement all the systems for client management.

Simply rinse and repeat for each area of law you want to cover.

STEP 3: LIMIT YOUR WORK AND FREE UP YOUR TIME

The less work you do, the more staff you have, the less profitable you are. This is what stops most attorneys from delegating to staff.

However, that thinking literally dooms most attorneys to a life of misery. Ironically, at the same time they end up making less money by trying to save.

Firstly, by streamlining how your practice is run, the staff you have right now can do more with the time they have. Everyone becomes more efficient.

This effectively gives you another member of staff without needing to hire anyone.

Secondly, you need to be more selfish with your time. If you are billing $200 per hour for your time, every single hour you can free up is saving you money.

For example, by getting your assistant, who gets paid $15–20 per hour, to prepare a lot of the paperwork, you have cut costs by 90%.

It cost your firm $20 instead of $200. Remember, your time matters just as much as your staff. You have to account for it.

Thirdly, being able to remove yourself from tasks means you can focus on growing.

Knowing how to run a law firm without you needing to be present is the golden goose.

Getting other attorneys to do your legal work for you is a great step in that direction. Yes, you do give away profits; however, you make up for it in volume.

For example, if your law firm makes a profit of $200,000 per year, bringing on another attorney would cost you about half that.

So now, your income has been cut by $100,000. That sounds awful, doesn't it?

Yet, since you reduced your costs with systems, you can offset the vast majority of that.

Also, you can handle double the number of clients. Now, all of a sudden, with the same amount of effort you can reach a profitability of $400,000–600,000 per year.

But that includes you working your butt off like you used to.

Removing yourself and having three to four offices will give you more money for less work.

Having ten to twelve offices will put you far into the millions, without you needing to be present. All of it well worth it if you ask me.

Don't be afraid to get top notch attorneys who are expensive to work for you. Remember, technically you aren't paying them; the client is. Financing will make it easy for clients to afford your new high-performing attorney.

In the next chapter, we're going to look at some of the systems. We've looked over checklists in a previous chapter, but this time we'll specifically look at them as assets that will help you to streamline and offload work.

If all you did was use a system to streamline your law firm to save thousands every year, even if you didn't grow, would it be worth it?

If all you did was use a system to make your life easier, would it be worth it?

If all you did was use a system to double your income, would it be worth it?

My point is you don't to become a huge, statewide law firm with millions in your bank account. You can simply use this stuff to be more profitable with what you've already got.

However, it is an astonishing way to grow and gain financial freedom.

CHAPTER 13

The "Lazy Attorney's" 6-Step Blueprint to Riches

"People who are unable to motivate themselves must be content with mediocrity, no matter how impressive their other talents."

Andrew Carnegie (1835–1919), Industrialist and founder of Carnegie Steel

ATTORNEYS ARE ABOUT to fall into the same trap as a man named Al Hafed. I don't want you to be one of them.

Hafed lost everything and was being swept away by the sea to his death. He was dressed in rags and hadn't eaten in weeks.

A few short years before, he had a farm and a family and was content with his life. He lived on the banks of the River Indus, the largest river in Asia. The river provided him with everything he needed—or so he thought.

Everything changed when an old priest visited him. The priest described how the world was made, including the riches the earth has to offer.

Precious metals and stones lay scattered around the globe. People often use them to enrich themselves. If you have just a few diamonds, you can have many farms, not just one.

Hafed, not so content with his life anymore, sold all his land to a younger man. He searched for diamonds across Persia, Palestine, and into Europe.

As the years went by, what money he had was all gone.

He was wandering around cities in rags and became a beggar.

One day, the current of the sea took him, and he didn't even fight it. He simply let it happen.

Meanwhile, the young man on the farm was watering his animals in a stream that ran through the property. Something quickly caught his eye.

There was a shiny object in the sands of the stream. It was a diamond. This diamond ended up being one of the richest finds in history. As it turns out, the mines of Golconda would yield not just one, or two, but acres of diamonds.

Attorneys up and down the country are falling into this same trap.

Think about where you are right now. Go on, *do it.*

Look around the room and notice where you are and what you are doing.

You have acres of diamonds in your possession; all you need to do is cash them in.

Your law office is your farm on the banks of the river. Right now, you may be getting enough from your farm to get by.

However, right underneath all of the carrots and the potatoes are diamonds.

Don't be like Hafed and go looking far and wide for riches and success. Everything you need is right underneath you. Either you take it, or another attorney will.

This book has given you the mining equipment you need in order to get to those diamonds.

Now it is up to you to use it. It is *your* responsibility.

But where do you begin?

There is a lot of information in this book, and if you feel over-whelmed, don't worry. It is totally natural.

In this short and final chapter, I am going to tell you exactly where to start.

You'll know with absolute certainty what your next step should be if you follow my instructions. So whatever you do, keep reading.

Remember, the waves of change are coming. You simply cannot avoid them.

Like the 200,000 handlooms in England who got swept away, so will attorneys be swept away.

There are too many attorneys and too few jobs. The employment rate for lawyers in America has fallen by 5%, while the rest of the economy has grown.

A wave of hundreds of thousands of younger lawyers will be leaving their corporate jobs to open local law offices. They will do anything and everything to steal your clients.

More and more work will be automated and given over to supercomputers.

You cannot escape it, but you can embrace the new strategies and technology available to you.

You can join the super attorneys, who are going to benefit a great deal from these changes, where you snap up all the clients while working less.

"Ok, I get it Gary, let's get started."

STEP 1

The very first step is to set up financing for your clients.

Do this at **EasyRetainer.legal**

People cannot afford to pay out of pocket for attorney fees. If your competition gets hold of this before you do, then you might as well kiss your law firm goodbye.

If people have the option between forking over thousands up front or just a few hundred dollars, they will pick the latter every single time.

The attorneys who don't do this will face a smaller and shrinking pool of clients.

By the time they realize that they should implement financing, they will have been outgrown by their local competitors. It will be too late.

Car companies that didn't offer financing when it became available went out of business quickly.

Up until recently, attorneys couldn't offer it because of bar rules. Now they can, so jump on board quickly.

STEP 2

Get a review system up and running. Ten years ago, it was the youth who relied on reviews. Now it is the older generation as well.

Eighty-eight percent of people trust an online review as much as a personal recommendation.

Right now, having reviews *win clients*. That's a well-known fact. However, little known to most is that reviews will become a requirement in the next few years.

Google is working on a system that will send a push notification to your phone with information about the firm you are visiting.

In other words, if you have no reviews, or just a few, the client sitting in your office will know. Google will notify them of it.

STEP 3

Use automation to follow up with potential clients.

This will save you time and grow your firm. People forget to call back all the time, even if they mean to.

In a lot of cases, they will simply contact another attorney because they forgot who you were.

Simple automated emails and texts go a long way. I have given you some basic starting templates. Use them yourself or outsource them.

STEP 4

Use high-ROI advertising to fill your pipeline with fresh new clients who are ready to pay.

Use the "problem first" approach to advertising to outwit and outsmart your competition.

Use the Passive Return Agents to get back prospects by positioning yourself as the authority.

STEP 5

Use cheat sheets and checklists to systemize everything you do at your firm.

Your staff will know exactly what to do when specific situations arise. Let your law firm run like a well-oiled machine when you are not around, rather than something that needs your close attention at all times.

STEP 6 (OPTIONAL)

Dominate one practice area at a time, and grow into one of the largest law firms in your state.

The reason I put this step as "optional" is because you don't need to take it that far. You can simply be a highly profitable small firm if you like. There is nothing wrong with that.

Or you can simply have two to three offices that can run without you. Selling these practices to other attorneys will be very easy when you are ready to retire. Especially if they run without you needing to be present.

THE LAZY WAY… and my damning admission

There you have it. All the steps, *oversimplified*, for your pleasure.

However, most super attorneys don't do those steps. Some of them don't even know about them.

Yet they are still going to thrive during the coming waves of change.

How?

Well, the answer to that question is the secret weapon most attorneys hate hearing.

They outsource it and listen to the experts.

Attorneys don't go to business school or marketing schools. They go to law school.

Attorneys don't spend all day testing out different strategies for button colors, headline text, intake procedures, or advertising innovations.

Nor should they.

You wouldn't expect a doctor to do his own legal work.

Even though that doctor is very good at what he does, he cannot possibly know everything there is to know about the legal system. And even if he did, he wouldn't have the time.

The same is true for you.

Even if you learned every single thing you could about the topics in this book, you probably don't have the time to implement everything.

That's why I am giving you my…

"Lazy Attorney's Guide to Growing Your LawFirm Without Spending a Penny"

Here's what I suggest.

Set up financing and start using it properly. This will free up a lot of cash.

Then, use that cash to outsource the rest of the steps outlined in this book.

So, the Lazy Attorney's Guide can be broken down into two simple steps.

1. You don't lose any money.

2. You make a hell of a lot more money.

There you have it.

Now, if you are still a little confused as to where you should start, I am going to throw in a bonus that'll make the next step an absolute no brainer.

You can have a free one-on-one "no-pitch" consultation with my company.

In other words, we will help you—without pitching you on our services—for free.

All you have to do is go to **BigMouthMarketing.co/book**.

Pick a time slot that works with your schedule, and book yourself in.

Now, why on this green earth would I offer you a free, no-pitch, consultation?

If there isn't a pitch in there, why am I doing it? What's the benefit to me?

The simple answer is that *I do benefit*. A lot.

The consultation finds out everything we need to so that we can tell you what to do.

A number of attorneys then come back to us and ask us to grow their law firm for them.

Essentially, we prove to you that we can help you by actually helping you. This is the problem first approach in action.

We will help you to solve your problem without expecting

anything in return, and that is how I run my business. It serves me very well, and it serves you even better.

So, go to **BigMouthMarketing.co/book** before all of the slots are taken up by other attorneys. You have nothing to lose, yet everything to gain.

I'll leave you with the closing statement from Ken Hardison when our interview concluded.

> *"You've got to have a plan and you've got to execute and you've got to have a vision and you've got to have a purpose. Get people around you that have purpose, leverage your strengths, and delegate your weaknesses because you can't be great at everything.*
>
> *I think that's the big deal with lawyers. I'd say the biggest stumbling block I see is ego. They're scared to hire anybody smarter than they are because they want to be the kingpin. They also think they already know it all and none of us know it all.*
>
> *John Woods said something like, "It's when you know it all, that's when it gets fun." I think I know as much as anybody in the country and I still learn stuff every day, every week. I mean, it never ceases to amaze me that there's always something new around the corner and, you know, you cannot rest on your laurels and start believing your own press. I've seen some very prominent lawyers go bankrupt because they read their own press. And I'll finish up with this, never fall in love with your law firm, only with your clients."*

Closing Statement from Gary Musler

THOMAS A. EDISON once said, "*Most people miss opportunity because it is dressed in overalls and looks like work.*"

As an attorney, it is all too easy to stick with what you know. It is all too easy to let an opportunity pass you by.

In a lot of cases, it is because the opportunity to grow your law firm is too much work. You don't have the time to do it.

However, you now have a different opportunity. You have an opportunity to grow in the most efficient way possible.

Yes, it still requires a little bit of work, but most of the work has already been done for you.

Warren Buffet once famously said, "*Someone's sitting in the shade today because someone planted a tree a long time ago.*"

Now is the time to plant your tree so that you can sit in the shade in the future. Nobody else is going to plant that tree for you.

The time is always now. Tomorrow never comes, until it is here today.

> "*Now is the time. You know, I think that the message is the one that I consistently share, which is, you can really love your life as a lawyer. You can love your law practice. You can be so glad that you went to law school. Your law*

degree can be the most valuable asset that you have when you choose the right practice area, and when you learn to practice in the New Law Business Model way."

–Alexis Neely

About the Author

ORIGINALLY FROM CONNECTICUT, Gary Musler is now the CEO and owner of Big Mouth Marketing. He's overseen a team that has run over 100,000 online ads, generated approximately 1.5 million leads, and conducted more than 5,000 marketing tests. In the 1990s, Gary built a multi-million-dollar financial planning business with 143 sales people on his payroll. His system was so popular that it was even mentioned in *Newsweek*. The secret to his success lied in his dogged determination to test everything people could throw at him. The internet was becoming a hot commodity and Gary started testing every single ad platform, lead type, and website layout he could.

He quickly earned a reputation when he became the biggest affiliate for online universities, generating a staggering 5,000 leads per day for a single client. One day, an attorney called him and asked if he could help with his marketing. Gary decided to run a test. After a few iterations, it became a resounding success. Since that day, tens of thousands of attorneys have consumed his content to help grow their law firms.

He oversaw the creation of, what came to be known as, The Crocodile Close®. A marketing system for attorneys so powerful that it is spreading throughout America like wildfire.

He lives in Scottsdale AZ and loves his dog as much as he loves the Red Sox.

Visit **BigMouthMarketing.co** for more information.

Made in the USA
Lexington, KY
16 November 2019

57126103R00098